Help Your
Child
To Talk

Help Your Child To Talk

FRANCES EVESHAM

CASSELL

To my parents,
Jack and Flo Bussey,
with my love

Cassell Publishers Limited
Artillery House, Artillery Row
London SW1P 1RT

© Frances Evesham 1989

British Library Cataloguing in Publication Data

Evesham, Frances
  Help your child to talk.
  1. Children to 4 years. Speech skills.
  Development.
  I. Title
  401'.9

ISBN 0 304 31560 5

Typeset by August Filmsetting, Haydock, St Helens

Printed and bound in Great Britain by
Biddles Ltd., Guildford and Kings Lynn

Frontispiece: Reading with your child encourages language skills

Contents

Acknowledgements

My grateful thanks go chiefly to my husband, David, who not only encouraged me and sorted out my difficulties with the word processor, but also took the photographs.

Thank you also to Christopher, Philippa, Nicholas, Helen and Jennifer for playing the games and being photographed in the process, and to Margaret Evesham for her personal and professional support.

Teachers and other professionals may be interested in the Derbyshire Language Scheme. The games in this book called 'Busy Teddy' and 'Doll's Tea Party' are based on ideas developed in the scheme. Courses in its administration are organised by Derbyshire County Council.

Introduction

The ability to talk is something that we tend to take for granted. We all talk every day, to our families and our friends, at work or when out shopping. We talk about important things, or gossip, or tell jokes, but we rarely stop to wonder how we do it. It is part of our lives.

Occasionally, however, our speech may let us down. Have you ever forgotten a name, or failed to find the words to describe something, or muddled the sounds of a word? At these times, it may have occurred to you that talking is not as easy as it seems. Our children have to learn to talk, right from the beginning, and we want them to learn easily, happily and well. This is the time when we need to ask questions about how speech and language are learned. What are the processes involved? Why do some people learn more quickly and easily than others? Why do some children have difficulty? Is there anything we can do to help our own children along the path to good communication?

The intention of this book is to give you some answers to the first three questions, while the answer to the last question is a resounding yes, for there are many things that you can do to help your child learn to talk. You undoubtedly do many of them instinctively, without having to think about it. When you smile at and talk to your new baby, you are beginning to help him already. Every time you read him a story, or sing a nursery rhyme, or even when you are building bricks together, you are teaching him some of the skills that he needs to use to learn good speech. This book attempts to explain what these skills are, and to describe some of the ways you can help your own child to improve them by playing games.

Parents sometimes wonder if 'teaching' their child is something that should be left to the professionals, and are concerned that they might confuse their child by playing 'learning games'. However, as every single thing you do with your child is teaching him something, you are an expert already! You know your child better than anyone else, and you know what he enjoys. Through reading this book, you will gain a greater understanding of how children learn to talk and how the games you play can help in that process; you will also find games that you may not have thought of playing with your child. Whichever of the games you play together, you will do him no harm so long as both of you are enjoying yourselves, and so long as you never let him feel that he is being tested in any way. The games in this book are designed to be fun, and at the same time to teach very important language skills. You and your child can have fun together, and you will have the pleasure of knowing that you are helping to give him a good start on the way to learning to talk well.

* * *

Every author of books about children is faced with the choice of using 'he' or 'she'. Since in recent years the tendency has been to use 'she', I have decided to redress the balance by using 'he'. The text does, of course, apply equally to boys and girls!

1

Language

How does language develop?

We are all aware of the importance of communication in our daily lives. We use language constantly to each other, and without it we would not be able to enjoy a conversation or an argument, tell a joke or read a book, listen to a story or carry a message. We would be cut off from much of our cultural heritage.

Children need to use language to make sense of the world they live in. By putting words to the things they see, feel and hear, they are able to understand new experiences in the light of previous ones. This enables them not only to talk about and ask for the things they need but also, later, to use language to think and plan, to regulate their own behaviour and to express their emotions.

Language is a precious ability which, it is widely accepted, is programmed into our genetic make-up. This means that your child is born with the potential to learn language and is receptive to the influences that help him to develop his own system of communication, be it English or Chinese. Although he is learning language from 'scratch', he starts with a big advantage.

This does not mean, however, that he cannot be helped enormously by being taught certain basic skills essential to the use of language, and in fact if he is not presented with sufficient opportunities to learn language, he will fail to develop it beyond a very rudimentary level.

The best people to help a child to learn language, especially in the very early stages, are those with whom he has very close emotional links. This will usually mean his parents or whoever is caring for him on a daily basis. He will learn most easily in a relaxed, happy home environment, where he feels close enough to an adult to be guided by that adult.

This essential emotional contact begins in the earliest days of

Communication in a 4-month-old baby: looking into her mother's eyes, she coos and gurgles

your baby's life, when you hold him, cuddle him, play with him and look into his eyes, establishing eye-contact with him. When you do this, the two of you are communicating with each other. Similarly, although he cannot talk, run or sit, or even smile at you, his shrieks and wails of hunger or discomfort tell you when he needs something, whilst his contented coos tell you that his wants are satisfied. Again, he is communicating with you.

From this point on, his language changes and grows through various stages in an ordered and systematic way. It may seem random and disorganised, but this is because each child is different, and his development is affected by many factors, including such things as his general health, hearing or eyesight. However, the order of development will be pretty much the same for most children. I will be discussing the things that might affect the rate of development of your child's language in the next section of this chapter.

He must, then, go through the following stages on the road to gaining a mastery of language. First, his crying will change so that after a few weeks you may be able to recognise a 'hungry' cry as opposed to a 'tired' cry, and fairly soon he will produce his first smile. This will most likely be at about six weeks, although it may be earlier, as there is always a certain amount of disagreement amongst parents, grandparents, etc. as to what is a smile and what is 'wind'! However, this smile whenever it occurs is of the utmost importance as it is a really obvious piece of communication, and it will spur you on to renewed efforts of smiling at and talking to your baby, which will in turn speed his language development along.

Of course, what you are really waiting for is the first recognisable word from your baby, but there are one or two other things he must learn first. At about six months he will start to 'babble' – that is, to play with sounds, repeating them and listening to them. 'Ba-ba' or 'da-da' are fairly typical examples of this stage, and it can be quite delightful to watch your child enjoying himself, practising the sounds that he is going to use soon in his first words. You can help at this point by joining in with the game, losing your inhibitions and babbling back. Your baby will look up and giggle at you, and renew his own efforts. Babbling back to your child should take place alongside, rather than instead of, talking to him normally. It is a game for you both to play, looking into each other's faces and having fun.

Then he will progress to copying words, or at least sounds that might just possibly be words, given a little imagination on your part. This will probably happen when he is about nine months old. When he says 'ma' do not be deterred by anyone who tells you it is just coincidence, or that he is too young to be saying 'mummy'. Show him how delighted you are, repeat it back and tell him what a clever boy he is. It will soon become the real thing. When he is between twelve and eighteen months he will most likely be producing one or two words that are obviously intended as such and cannot be put down to coincidence.

Now, these first words are a real milestone, but it is very important to realise that plenty of language ability has already been acquired to make those words possible. Remember, understanding must come first. He will not use one word until he has a good understanding of many more. You will probably have noticed him gradually responding more and more to the things you say to him. This may begin when you realise he is turning to look for his cup when he hears you say 'drink', or looking at the cupboard when you say 'biscuit'. Encourage this new understanding by congratulating him as soon as you notice his responses.

When his first words appear, possibly 'ma-ma' or 'da-da', although it could just as well be the cat's or dog's name, do not stop talking nonsense and babbling with your child, because it is vital that both you and he enjoy yourselves. And don't forget animal noises, or the noises of his toy cars – it is all good practice for him. There is more about this in the chapter on Speech Sounds.

Meanwhile, you will notice that because his understanding (comprehension) is always ahead of his speech (expressive language) he will use one word to mean a whole phrase or idea. Thus, his 'ma-ma' may mean a whole range of things, from 'I want mummy' to 'Mummy give me a drink.' You will usually find that you can understand what he means.

From this point on, your child's language will not proceed smoothly, but in fits and starts, as he first learns to understand new types of words and then incorporates them into his own speech. This often causes a certain amount of anxiety as he apparently stops increasing his vocabulary for a few weeks at a time, but if you remember the sequence of comprehension first, followed a little later by expression, you will be able to recognise progress in his language, even if you can't hear it in his words.

You can at the same time see how he is learning to understand the world around him in many ways. This begins with his realising that a door that is closed may be opened so that he can go through it, and that an object may remain where it has been put even if he can no longer see it. Try this out for yourself, by letting him watch you put a handkerchief over one of his toys, then asking him to find the toy. In the early months he will not look for it under the handkerchief, but one day, probably during his second year, he will know where it is and find it. As he learns the names of things, talking about them will help him to continue this process of understanding.

The first words that your child uses will probably be nouns, that is, the names of things, because these words are the most useful to him in getting what he wants and because you will have been repeating more of these than any other kind of word to him. Next, he will move on to verbs, or 'action' words, and by 24 months he will be using a few of these, although not necessarily in conjunction with his nouns. It is quite possible that he will still be using single words at this age, and this is definitely not a sign that there is anything wrong.

By three years, he will have begun to use adjectives and adverbs, and then prepositions, pronouns and conjunctions will follow over the next year or so. The table in figure 1 will remind you what these different parts of speech are.

As with all developmental activities, language will be learned at different rates by different children, so there is no point in comparing your child with anyone else's, or even with another of your own offspring. To do so is a sure way of introducing anxiety.

However, at any time during these years, you may feel that your child is falling behind in his language learning. If so, do get in touch with a speech therapist rather than sit at home worrying, and possibly making your child anxious. There is a

Figure 1
Some parts of speech

Part of speech	Description	Examples
Noun	a name	cup food mummy
Verb	an action	to jump to cry to have
Adjective	a description of a noun	a *big* hat a *happy* smile
Adverb	a description of a verb	to sing *loudly* to walk *slowly*
Preposition	a place or position	in under between
Pronoun	a replacement for a noun	me her it
Conjunction	links two parts of a sentence	but and however

6

common misconception that there is no point in seeing a therapist until a child is three or so, but this is definitely not the case, and referrals can be made at any age. Have a word with your doctor or health visitor, who will tell you how to get to see the therapist and will probably refer you straight away. It is especially important to see a speech therapist if you feel that your child may be having difficulty in understanding language.

What influences a child's language development?

I have already mentioned that there are many factors that influence how quickly and successfully a child learns language. Some of these are obvious, but there are several more hidden influences on a child, and if a parent is aware of these it can help her understand the differences in language learning between children who may seem at first to be alike. Sometimes it is possible to do something about a circumstance that is having a bad effect on a child's learning.

There is, of course, the obvious fact that some people have an in-built potential to handle language better than others. It is foolish to deny that we have a certain genetic make-up, inherited from our parents, and that in some people this includes all the characteristics which go towards becoming extra skilful with language. Into this category go the great wordsmiths. Shakespeare or Wordsworth, John Betjeman or Ted Hughes, all these must have been blessed with 'all the right genes'. On the other hand, there are plenty who have other abilities which are destined by nature to be better than their language abilities. However, apart from such tragedies as brain damage, whether from accident or as part of an innate medical syndrome, we are all born with the potential abilities to learn to use language adequately. Whether or not a child will gain his full potential depends, of course, on the other factors which will influence his language development.

If a child is to gain ground in any aspect of his learning, his general health must be reasonably good. Any child who

7

constantly suffers from poor health will find it difficult to summon up the energy and enthusiasm to listen attentively to what is going on around him, so he will not pick up new words, expressions or uses of language. At the same time he will not feel like experimenting with his own use of words, and his self-expression will suffer. If poor health is a constant state for a child, it is unreasonable to expect his learning to progress as quickly as it would otherwise. In any case, if your child suffers from constant ill health, his language development is unlikely to be at the top of your list of worries. It is, however, worth remembering that if your child has been suffering from a rather prolonged spate of colds, chicken pox etc., you will probably not notice much improvement in his language until he has returned to full strength.

It is vital for a child to be able to understand language before he can learn to use it. Before comprehension can take place it is, of course, necessary that he can hear what is being said to him, so any child who is suffering from a hearing problem is bound to have some difficulty in acquiring language. Sometimes the hearing problem may not be noticed, particularly if it fluctuates, and poor speech and language may be the first indication that there is anything wrong. Some children suffer from quite severe hearing losses when they have colds, and if this happens very frequently it can prevent language development from proceeding as smoothly as it should. In some of these cases, the children may have passed their baby hearing tests, having been free of colds on that day, so if you suspect your child may have this problem it is well worth discussing it with your doctor or health visitor. It is well to bear in mind that all children (and adults) can suffer from a temporary deafness with a cold, and it is a good idea to make sure that you are speaking especially clearly to your child at these times, without, of course, shouting in his ear!

When considering your child's language development, it is very important to remember that it is not the only thing that he is learning during his early years. He is also struggling to gain control of his body, to sit, crawl and walk, to feed himself and to manipulate toys. It would be unreasonable to expect all these new activities to develop smoothly and regularly. Each has an effect on the others, with the result that language learning may take a back seat for a while when, for example, your child has just learned to crawl and is off exploring his new world, or if he has discovered the delights of putting things in boxes and taking them out again. This activity can occupy almost every waking moment of a child's day when it is a new skill. At these times, there is no point in trying to force your child to pay attention to new language, as you will both become frustrated. Be patient, wait for the sudden interest in language which will come in time, and take advantage of that by listening and talking to your child and praising him when he joins in.

If you can learn to be sensitive to the times when your child is interested in learning new words and phrases, you will be able to do a great deal to help him to achieve his full potential in language. Much has been written and said about providing a 'stimulating environment' for your child, and many parents who are truly anxious to help their child to do well interpret this advice as meaning that they must talk constantly to him, point out and name everything they see and provide a permanent barrage of conversation. Unfortunately, this over-stimulation usually has the effect of making the child mentally 'tune out', and he therefore learns less than the child whose parents are selective in what they say to him. After all, it is the same as bombarding the average adult with a lecture on an obscure scientific topic, using words that he has never heard before. It would not be long before he lost concentration and gazed out of the window instead. A child's ability to concentrate is less than an adult's and he will accordingly pay no attention at all. On the other hand, when he shows interest in language, you should seize the opportunity to encourage him. Make sure that the things you say to him, and the games you play, are things that interest him rather than you!

The question of how much language a child hears, and whether or not it is suited to his level of understanding, comes up again when you consider your child in relation to the other children in the family. Your first child has the advantage of getting most of his language stimulation from adults, especially from the person who looks after him the most, whether it be his mother, father or another person. He may, though this is not always the case, learn to talk early and well, depending on the other factors influencing him. The second child, however, although born into the same family with parents who are just as anxious for him to do well, has to deal also with his older brother or sister talking all the time and at a higher level than he can. This child is therefore likely to be at some disadvantage in his own language learning. The third child, of course, has even more difficulty in finding someone who talks at his level, and may have a battle to get his voice heard and to practise any words he manages to learn.

It is worth thinking about conversations in your own house, and consider which child does the most talking in everyday situations, such as in the car or at the breakfast table. It is so easy to carry on a conversation with the child whose language is most mature and who is therefore nearest to the parents' level, at the expense of the other children.

Of course, it is not always a disadvantage to a child to have older brothers and sisters, as they may often provide a good deal of language stimulation themselves, in a far less self-conscious way than parents. A child with older siblings often experiences a much wider range of activities, visiting friends, playgroups, or simply going on more outings to the seaside or country. The child's position in the family is important in relation to his language development, and a careful parent will, with a little thought, see where the advantages or disadvantages to a particular child lie, so that she can then rectify matters, for example, by instituting a system of 'taking turns' to talk from time to time, to ensuré that the poorer speaker does not always have to fight it out unaided with his siblings.

There is, interestingly, a marked difference between the sexes in speed and efficiency of acquiring language, as girls tend to learn language more quickly than boys. In fact, there are about four times as many boys as girls referred to the speech therapy clinics. There is not much a parent can do about this, but it is another valid reason for not trying to compare one child with another.

These, then, are some of the factors which can have an influence on your child's ability to acquire language quickly and successfully. By being aware of them you can help your child to overcome some potential disadvantages, and give him the best possible chance of learning to talk. It is a good idea to consider the skills and abilities that he must learn on the way to becoming a good communicator, because it is by encouraging the improvement of these, as well as by providing a good environment and talking to him at the right level, that you can help him to improve.

If you feel that your child needs to improve any of these abilities, and in fact most children can benefit from extra practice in most of them, try some of the games and activities which are outlined in the games chapter. If you are reading this book because you are really concerned that your child has a language problem, then go to see a speech therapist to discuss it. Don't try to diagnose any real problem yourself, for however competent you may feel, an outside specialist will see a much clearer picture of your child than you possibly can.

What language abilities does your child need?
One of the most important skills that a child must learn, if he is to have any hope at all of acquiring language successfully, is that of attending to what he hears. I have been stressing all along that understanding is the first step towards using speech, and the child who cannot concentrate on one thing at a time is

obviously not going to be able to understand or remember things that he hears.

A young baby has no control over his own attention. He hears a noise, and looks towards it, then he is distracted by another and loses interest in the first. However, even at a few weeks of age he begins to try to attend to one type of noise, for example, his mother's voice, in preference to another noise. This selectiveness of attention needs to grow so that he learns to listen to what is being said to him even if there is the noise of a car in the background, or somebody walking nearby. You can encourage this in a tiny baby by catching his eye, when you are playing with and cuddling him, and smiling at him to hold his attention for a few moments.

A toddler or young child who seems unable to settle down to play with one toy, who constantly flits from one activity to another, and who never listens long enough to hear what you are saying is probably finding it difficult to control his own attention, and will need to learn to do this as soon as possible. If you keep your eyes open, you will find ways of helping him to keep his attention where he needs it to be. For example, try to cut out distractions when you have something to say to him. Turn the television or radio off, say his name and wait until he is looking at you before you speak. This will ensure that you have his full attention, and he will be far more likely to understand you and do as he is told. However, do beware of getting annoyed, shouting his name or looking angry when he does look at you. These reactions will not encourage him to turn his attention to you next time.

Similarly, when you are playing with him, or even just keeping an eye on him while he plays, try to encourage him to play a little longer with a toy instead of casting it aside in favour of another after a few seconds. You could, for example, indicate something about a toy that he may not have noticed, or suggest a different way of using the toy. Toys such as bricks are wonderful for this sort of attention training, as you can build them

Removing other distractions helps your child to concentrate on the game in hand

in towers, bridges, lines; group them according to colour, size or shape; or just hide them in boxes and pull them out one at a time to talk about. Make sure that, when he is playing with one toy, he is not surrounded by dozens of others, as these will be a distraction.

You can show your child how he can use language to help plan his own actions. For example, if you are playing with a ball together it may roll out of reach. On his way to fetch it your child may be distracted by something else. You can remind him to 'Get the ball', so that he turns his attention back to the original object. When he has a sufficient fund of words himself, he will talk in order to direct his own activities. It is common to hear toddlers talking to themselves when they are playing, saying, 'Where's yellow pencil?', 'Put paper in middle' and so on. They will gradually learn to internalise this so that they do not have to say the words out loud, and will finally reach the adult stage of thought. Your direction of your child's early activities lays the foundation for these processes by showing him how it is done.

Whilst your child is playing like this, he may become very engrossed in what he is doing, and you may find he is unable to listen to your suggestions or comments on his game. At these times it is best to play alongside him, rather than telling him what to do, and gradually to join in with his game. Let him be in charge of the activities if he wishes.

Along with an ability to control his own attention, your child needs the ability to concentrate for a reasonable length of time on whatever it is he has turned his attention to. His concentration span increases as his understanding of language improves, so that he can listen to an instruction, joke or story without losing interest or attention. You can make this easier for him by adjusting the length of what you are saying so that he is able to concentrate fully while you are saying it. If he is only able to take in two words at a time, then only use two at a time to begin with, and then gradually introduce three from time to time.

Don't make everything you say to him so difficult that he is always having to work hard to understand you, but keep to his level most of the time and then, just occasionally, stretch him.

Once your child is able to attend to what you say and concentrate long enough to take in the whole of it, he will need to make use of another ability before the information will be of much use to him. He will have to remember it long enough to act on it. There are different types of memory, from the long-term memory of years ago which remains with the very elderly, to the short-term memory of the last few seconds. Without a good short-term memory, of course, a child will not retain the information he has just heard long enough to make use of it. It is also important to language development that he is able to remember sounds, words and phrases in the right order, which we call the ability to 'sequence'. There are very few people, whether children or adults, who could not improve their memory to advantage, and children of all ages enjoy games which test their memories.

A most important feature of language, which is often not recognised, is that it is a sophisticated way of using symbols. This fact is overlooked because the symbols used are heard and spoken, rather than seen and written. Nevertheless, a word is an abstract thing which stands for an object, an action, an idea etc., and so a child will not be able to use language if he cannot understand its symbolic nature.

This is one of the reasons why a child takes a long time to learn to talk, as the ability to understand symbols is gradually acquired. He moves from a total lack of awareness of anything outside himself, which is his state at birth, to seeing that objects exist around him. He learns that one chair may look different from another, but that it is nevertheless a similar kind of thing, and then that a toy chair is a 'pretend' chair, or a symbol for a chair, and that a picture of a chair is another symbol. In the same way, he has to learn that a collection of sounds (a word) can also mean a chair.

It will help your child to acquire new words if you point out to him all the different ways things can be represented. When you play with your child, relate toys to the real world, for example, by comparing a toy cup with a real one, then pointing out pictures of cups. Teddies and dolls are of enormous use for this – in fact, you may find your toddler trying to feed his teddy, or make it walk. Encourage this, for he is exploring how a real thing can be represented by a toy. The games chapter describes several games you can play to expand this learning.

As well as learning that toys, pictures and words can stand for objects, a child also learns that things can be grouped together in various ways. They can be grouped according to use: for example, things we eat go together, or different forms of transport; or they can be grouped by colour, or size, or according to where they are found. This ability to make associations between things enables a child to increase and enrich his language, and must exist before he can produce original sentences. If this ability is poor, his language will tend to be rather stereotyped and unoriginal and he will find it of limited use.

He will learn to make these associations, not by your presenting him with objects and telling him their names, but by experiencing the different aspects of things and grouping them in various ways. This process can lead to him making many mistakes, because he will not always see the same similarities between things that an adult can see. He may, for example, learn the word 'daddy' for his own father, but then may use the word to mean any man, or indeed he may use it for anything nice, such as a favourite toy. This is because he is recognising some of the attributes of his 'daddy' but not all of them. This phase will soon pass as his experience grows.

Another form of symbolisation which often accompanies language learning is the use of gesture. Babies learn to point at what they want before they are able to ask for it, and they sometimes develop quite elaborate systems of gesture, especially if they are finding it difficult to use words – perhaps because they have trouble with making the sounds involved in speaking. Problems of phonology, as the process of making speech sounds is called, are dealt with more fully in the next chapter, but if your child is using a great deal of gesture, remember that at least he is using some form of language, even if it is non-verbal, and let him make himself understood in this way, whilst at the same time using the correct words yourself. Ignoring your child's gestures on the grounds that he should be using words will only lead to frustration and misery all round, although it would not hurt occasionally to 'misunderstand' a gesture, just to see if he will produce a word, however poorly spoken, instead.

How to talk to your child

The improvement of any of the language skills mentioned here can only have a beneficial effect on your child's communication, and playing language games can be a very enjoyable activity for both of you, so long as you remember that the operative word here is 'games'. Effective language learning should be full of fun, whilst the child who is constantly told 'say "dog"' will see the whole business as unhappy and difficult, and his abilities will suffer as a result. This is one of the essential rules when talking to your child, whether you are trying to teach new words or simply chatting with him. You feed him the information, perhaps by saying 'Look at the dog,' and let him look. When he has heard the word 'dog' several times, used with different dogs, with a soft toy, perhaps with small models of dogs, and with pictures in books, he will venture the word himself.

At this point, your reaction is of vital importance. If his attempt at 'dog' is 'o', be pleased, praise him for knowing what the word is – after all, you will realise how many skills and how much understanding have gone into the production of that attempt. Say 'Yes, it's a dog' and smile or give your child a kiss, so that he knows you appreciate his cleverness. Never criticise his early attempts to talk. It is heartbreaking to hear a child who is trying his first few words being told 'Not "o", "dog".' At this stage of development any attempt at using words is good. There is no need to worry about the sounds in these early stages.

Whilst you are encouraging him and reinforcing what he has said by this correct repetition, it can be very helpful to expand his word or sentence a little. Make some other remark about the dog such as 'Look at his big ears!' which will widen the conversation a little. Do beware, however, of taking over the conversation and talking too much. It is not a good idea to flood your child with too much language which he may not be able to assimilate, as this might leave him feeling puzzled rather than pleased with himself for knowing the right word. Just say enough to let him hear an extra idea which he can incorporate into his awareness of what a 'dog' can be.

If you feel your child is 'reluctant' to talk, perhaps because he feels that everyone is listening too hard to his performance, try to take the pressure off him. For example, when looking at a book with him, talk about the things you see without expecting him to name them. You could say, 'Look, there's a little boy, and there's his house,' rather than 'What's that?' After a while you will find him joining in, but still avoid behaving as though you are listening closely to every word. Say, 'There's a . . . ' and pause, to give him a chance to say the word. If he does try it, say 'Yes, that's right' and carry on without making a fuss. If he does not say the word, just fill it in yourself and continue. Your attitude should be one of giving him a chance to talk, being pleased if he does, but not upset if he does not.

Try always to be positive in your attitude to your child's attempts at talking, and correct him by repeating his words as they should be, as you praise him. Resist the temptation to ask him to repeat them correctly, as this is thoroughly boring for him, and he will get it wrong anyway, so that a pleasant experience will turn into a bad one.

In the same way, you can teach him a great deal by giving him a good example to follow. Try to talk clearly and reasonably slowly when you are with him, although do beware of overdoing this. Neither he nor you should feel that you put on a 'special voice' when you talk to him.

When you are talking to your child, it helps if you bear in mind the level of language that he can understand. This will be in advance of what he is saying because he will always be able to understand more than he can say, but you should try to avoid constantly using sentences which are very long and involved. He will not understand enough to be able to retain the information, and may become confused. It is not so difficult as it sounds to do, and most people automatically cut down their own language level to that of the child without realising that they are doing it. The best way to guard against using language that is too difficult is to notice your child's reaction. If he loses interest in what you are saying, or gets it wrong, you have probably made things too complicated. For example, if you say to your two-year-old, 'Get your bib out of the drawer in the dining room and put it on the table,' you may get a puzzled look, or he may wander into the dining room and forget the rest of the instruction. If this is the case, make it simpler for him. You could say, 'Come into the dining room,' and accompany him there. Then say, 'Get your bib out of the drawer,' and when he has done that, tell him to 'Put it on the table.' You will probably find that he will manage all that and be thoroughly pleased with himself.

There is much controversy over whether or not you should use 'baby talk' to your child. I feel that this is a matter of personal taste, as it will do no harm if your child calls a horse a 'gee-gee', for by the time it would matter, at school for example, he will probably have learned its correct name. On the other hand, this does give him two words to learn instead of one! Use whichever words you feel happiest with, but do avoid teaching him words which are only used inside the family, as this can make him difficult to understand outside the home. It can be most unfortunate for a child at school who uses some obscure, coy expression for the toilet, because by the time his teacher has puzzled out what he is talking about, it may be too late.

Finally, do remember that, on the whole, children like to please you, and they enjoy experimenting with language. They are not 'lazy' with talking, but can only proceed at their own pace. They will make mistakes all the time, but you should see these as part of the learning process, and a sign that your child is trying to widen his horizons. Instead of being critical, try to praise, be positive and give a good example yourself.

2
Speech Sounds

Up to now I have talked mostly about how a child learns language because this is the first and most important aspect of talking. It is not enough, however, for him to know what words he wants to say, he must also be able to make the sounds which form each word and to link the sounds together correctly. Of course, when he is only two or three years old, no one expects to be able to understand everything he says, although his parents can usually make a good guess at most of it. Gradually, though, his system of sounds should show signs of becoming more like that of an adult, in spite of the many mistakes he will make along the way.

It is well worth considering exactly how a child learns which sounds he needs to use, and how to fit them together, for it is not at all a simple process. It can often be irritating for a parent when a child persists in making what seem to be obvious mistakes in speech, but an understanding of how difficult it is to learn sounds correctly makes it seem a greater mystery that any child ever gets his speech right than that he should make mistakes. Nevertheless, most children do achieve acceptable speech in the end.

For most of us, the ability to talk has become so much a part of us that we give very little thought to it. It is in many ways like learning to drive. At first, the processes of driving are unfamiliar and difficult to co-ordinate, but with practice they become so familiar that we no longer need to think about what we are doing. In the same way our speech becomes 'second nature' to us. We think of what we want to say, and then we say it. It is not until we begin to think about exactly what we are doing that we realise there is a great deal of well co-ordinated activity involved in the process of putting sounds together to make words. For example, if you take an apparently simple word, such as 'cat', and break it down into its separate sounds, then consider what you are doing with your lips and tongue (not to mention your palate and vocal cords) to make those sounds, you will realise just how tiny and precise the movements are.

To take the first sound, 'c'. In the International Phonetic Alphabet, which deals with sounds rather than spellings, this would be written [k]. In this book, anything written inside square brackets is a sound, not a letter, so [k] is the sound for 'c' in 'cat' rather than being pronounced 'kay'. Make the sound [k] yourself, several times, and try to feel what is happening in your mouth. Can you feel what your tongue is doing? If you find it difficult to identify the movements your 'articulators' (which is what we call the parts of the body involved in making sounds) are making, then try contrasting [k] several times with the sound at the end of the word 'cat', which happens to be written [t]. You should begin to feel your tongue performing a sort of rocking movement, as you use the tongue tip for [t] and the back of the tongue for [k]. Now try the other sound from the word, which is the vowel 'a'. Your tongue is fairly relaxed for this sound, but this time, consider what your lips are doing. Try making the sound with your lips pursed as if you were trying to say 'oo' and you will find that it is almost impossible. In this case, you are using your lips to help form the sound, although your tongue position is still important.

Say a few more words or single sounds, and see if you can tell what your tongue and lips are doing. For example, try 'pin', or 'dog'. Once you begin to be aware of the movements needed for different sounds, you will quickly see that to fit all these sounds together to make words and sentences involves a great number of rapid and precise movements. Then think about how much more complicated are the movements which have to be co-ordinated in words containing whole strings of consonants, all blended together. Say 'scratch' or 'freckle' to yourself and feel how hard your articulators are working. It is not surprising that children make many mistakes in learning sounds, nor is it strange that it takes years rather than months for a child's sound system or phonology to become fully mature.

Later in this chapter I shall be describing more of the similarities and differences between sounds and how they can be grouped together, but first it would be helpful to think about the factors that can affect a child's ability to learn sounds and how to put them together in words.

What influences the development of a child's phonology?

In the chapter on language, I talked about the many factors that have an influence on how quickly and well a child learns language. Similarly, there are many influences working on a child's speed and accuracy in developing his sound system, which means that each child will develop at his own rate. An understanding of the kinds of things that have a bearing on his learning of sounds will enable you to help him develop them as well as he is able.

One of the most important factors, so far as speech development is concerned, is whether or not a child can hear properly. This is one of the major factors affecting language, but it is even more vital to a child's sound system that he hears, not approximately, but exactly what is being said to him. It is possible for a child to manage to understand most of what is being said if he has a very slight hearing difficulty, but it is quite impossible for him to learn to recognise the tiny differences that are essential between, for example, [s] and [f] if he cannot really hear accurately what those differences are. You can understand this easily by talking and listening on the telephone, which cuts out some of the sounds which the human ear can detect, although there are enough sounds left for most of what is being said to be understood. However, there is often confusion over words such as 'fight' and 'sight'. For some children, who have slight hearing difficulties, this confusion happens all the time. These children often manage to compensate for their loss by watching very carefully the lips of the person who is talking to them, for this can supply vital clues to the sounds that seem the same to them. It is possible, for example, to tell the difference between [s] and [f] by watching, as in [f] the upper teeth are placed on the lower lip. Look in the mirror and try out the sounds yourself, and you will see the difference. Children with a slight hearing loss can become clever at lip-reading. Nevertheless, speech is complicated enough for them to learn, so that even the mildest hearing loss can cause quite dramatic confusions. Make sure, therefore, that your child has his hearing tested by the health visitor, and watch out for the tell-tale signs of hearing loss, such as his watching your face very closely when you talk, and turning from speaker to speaker in an exaggerated way when he is following a conversation. You may find he makes mistakes by misunderstanding what you are saying, or appears to ignore things you say. It is, of course, easy to confuse this type of behaviour with the ordinary kind of 'deafness' shown by all children when you say 'Go to bed'. However, if you have any worries about your child's hearing, do have a word with your health visitor and get things sorted out as soon as possible.

I have already mentioned that children use what they can see to compensate for what they are unable to hear, and it therefore follows that if a child has poor eyesight you will have to make allowances for this and make sure that he gets plenty of opportunity to look closely at your mouth when you are talking to him. In these cases, it can be helpful to let him feel what movements your mouth is making with his hands, and in fact it benefits any child to use his sense of touch to add to the information he gains from vision and hearing.

It would be nice if, having established that your child has not got a hearing problem, you could forget all about hearing so far as his sound system is concerned. Unfortunately, this is not possible because the differences between the sounds used in speech are so tiny that he must also have very well developed listening skills. I mentioned these in the chapter dealing with language, for the ability both to listen well and to remember what he has listened to, in the right order, are vital to language learning. However, his skills need to be even sharper if his language is to be enhanced by good, clear speech. In addition to the skills already mentioned, he must be able to detect the features of speech that make the word 'hat' sound different from the word 'had'. I will say more about these features later in this chapter, so don't worry if you can't put the differences into words. We call this ability 'auditory discrimination', and it is something that you can help your child to improve by playing some of the games in the games chapter of the book.

There are other hearing skills which a child needs if he is to be able to sort out what he is hearing in the speech of the people around him. This is because often when we talk we do not pronounce all the sounds in a word exactly as we would if we were saying the word on its own. We miss out bits of a word, or we glide sounds together, and your child needs to be able recognise what the word is, even if he can only hear part of it. For example, we rarely use the word 'and' in its complete form, but usually reduce it to 'an' or 'n', yet everyone knows what we mean.

Each sound is influenced by the sounds around it and can become quite unlike its usual form. For example, in the phrase 'white car', the sound [t] at the end of 'white' is often pronounced more like the [k] from the beginning of 'car'. Your child has to recognise that it is still the word 'white' whichever way it is spoken, or he will not learn to say it correctly himself. Again, people often leave out the [t] from the middle of words such as 'butter', especially if they speak with one of several regional accents, and a child has to be able to recognise what the word would have sounded like had he heard each sound pronounced individually. There are some games in the 'listening' portion of the games chapter that can improve his skill in this area.

If a child has perfect hearing and is learning good listening skills he will be able to tell what the sounds are that he is trying to make. He then needs to be able to use this knowledge to make the sounds himself. To be able to do this, he needs to have a good set of the physical equipment he will be using. This equipment consists mainly of his 'articulators' and includes lips and tongue and the roof of the mouth which is called the palate, while his jaw, teeth, tonsils and adenoids also have an effect on his speech. His vocal cords and breathing muscles are also involved, and there is more about these in the chapter dealing with Voice. It is probably helpful to take these articulators one at a time, and look at how they are used in speech and how efficient they need to be.

The lips are used for several consonants, including [p], [b] and [m], and also in all the vowel sounds. They are the organs that we notice most when we watch someone speaking, so they offer a big problem to amateur ventriloquists, who are forced to talk about 'gottles o' geer' to prevent their lips from moving. For speech the lips are sometimes pressed together tightly so that breath pressure builds up behind them, to be released in a small explosion as in [p], or they are at other times stretched wide as in the vowel 'ee' in the word 'see'. At other times again they are pursed up to make a small round gap, as in 'oo'. These different shapes are achieved by the actions of the muscles around the mouth, including those of the cheek. Anyone who has ever been to the dentist and had an injection of local anaesthetic will know how a lack of feeling in the lips and a lack of control over them make speech difficult.

The tongue is an organ of vital importance for speech, which

26

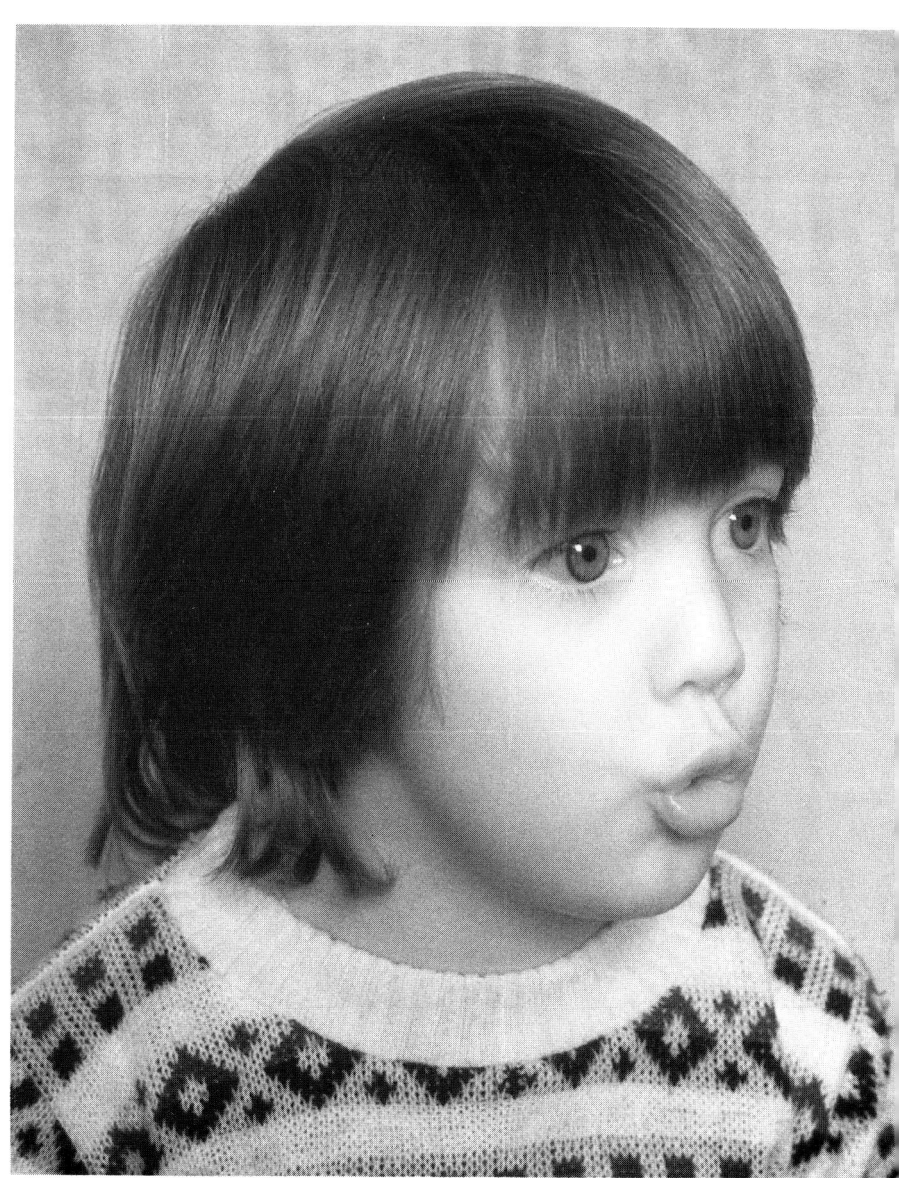

The lip shape for 'oo'

is why people sometimes talk about 'foreign tongues' when they mean foreign languages. It is a very muscular part of the body, and must move in many different ways to make a variety of sounds. The tip must be mobile, for it needs to move upwards to touch the ridge just behind the upper teeth, as in the sounds [t] and [d]. The whole tongue must bunch itself up so that the back can touch the palate, as in [k] and [g], the sides need to be raised independently of the tip for [s] and [z], and lowered independently for [l]. All these actions must take place in rapid succession in words, so a mobile tongue is an absolute essential for good speech. Some children appear to lack mobility in the tongue tip because their tongue is 'tied' by an unusually short frenum, which is the small piece of skin under the tongue. It is very rare for this 'tongue tie' to be severe enough to prevent adequate movement of the tongue, and operations to cut the frenum, which were quite common at one time, are hardly ever necessary. As the child grows, the tongue grows too, and the tongue tie normally disappears.

The palate stretches from the upper front teeth, right across the top of the mouth and ends in the uvula, which is the little piece of tissue that is visible hanging down at the back of the mouth. The front of the palate is hard and bony, does not move, and is there to divide the mouth from the nose. The back is called the soft palate, and this moves down so that air can pass between the nose and the passageways to the lungs, which is most useful for breathing. However, during most sounds apart from [m] and [n] the soft palate moves up so that no air passes from the air passageways to the nose. If the soft palate does not move well, or if it is not long enough to stop all the air from going up into the nose, or if the hard palate has a hole in it, all sounds will be affected by a nasal quality which can make speech almost unintelligible. When a baby is born, the midwife or doctor will always put her finger in his mouth, to test for a small hole or cleft, so it is most unlikely that your child has a cleft palate without your knowing about it.

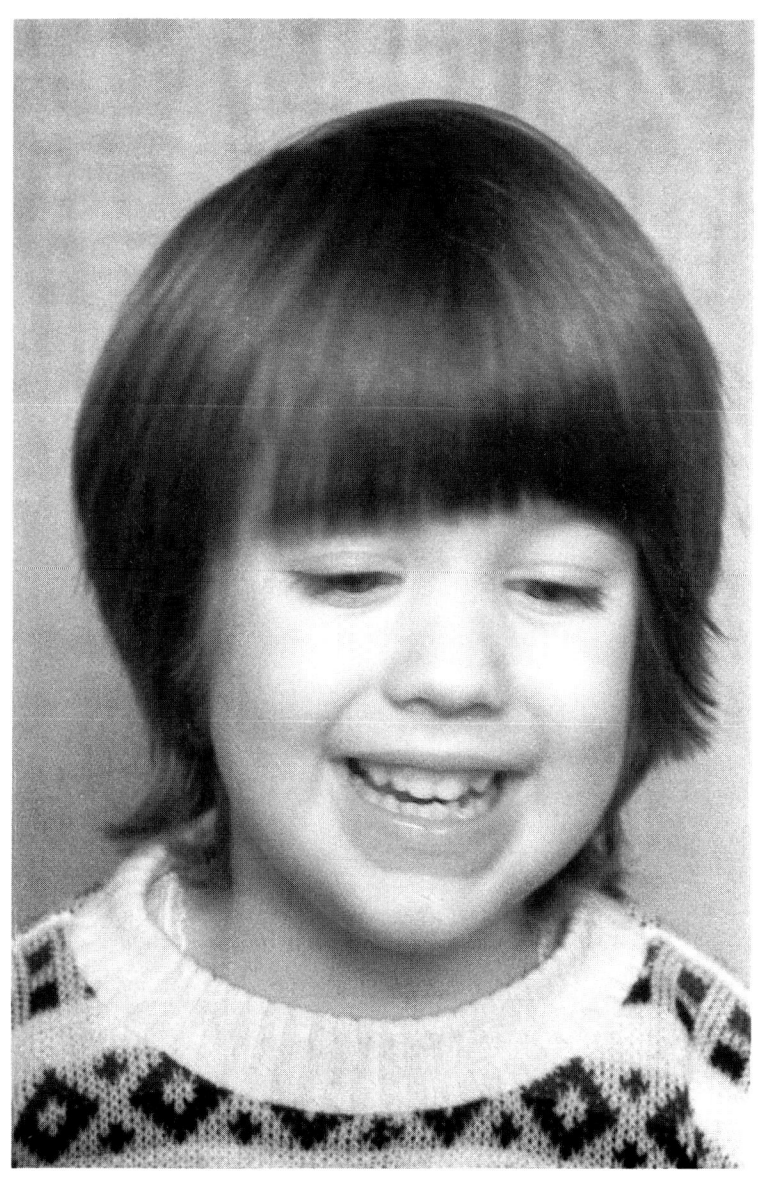

The lip shape for 'ee'

These are the main articulators, but speech can also be affected by other organs. The teeth and jaw can be of importance, as unusual jaw shapes or teeth can affect some sounds. Most people find that when they close their teeth together, their back teeth touch while their upper front teeth are in front of their lower front teeth, but there are variations on this arrangement which, while not making speech difficult to understand, can make it sound 'wrong'. If the upper teeth are too far in front of the lower teeth, the tongue may come too far forward for some sounds, notably the [s], and this can result in a 'lisp', while an unusually shaped jaw can encourage air to escape sideways on a [s] sound, producing what is commonly called a 'lateral s'. These small variations in sounds can often be corrected by practice, and your speech therapist is the best person to advise you on how to go about this. It would be a most unusual jaw formation which would prevent a child from being able to produce reasonably accurate speech.

The state of a child's tonsils and adenoids can also have a slight effect on the quality of his speech, as enlarged adenoids can stop air from passing between the nose and the air passageways, which will give a muffled quality to speech, especially on the [m] and [n] sounds. This is a similar effect to the one that we all experience when we have colds and our nasal passages are blocked. Enlarged adenoids are often temporary affairs, fortunately, which improve as a child grows older.

Although all these organs have an effect on a child's speech, there is no need to get too anxious about your child's articulators, as there is quite a wide range of what is normal. Everyone has slightly differently shaped lips, tongue, jaws and palate from everyone else, and this is partly why no one's speech sounds exactly like anyone else's. However, it is important that a child can use his speech equipment as well as possible, and there are simple exercises that he can enjoy which will give his articulators the necessary mobility for good speech.

The parts of the body that are used in speech are also the

parts that are used for eating and drinking, and as a child learns to feed long before he learns to talk, his feeding skills have a big influence on the way he uses his articulators. In fact, when a tiny baby begins to make sounds, the movements his articulators make are exactly those that he is using for feeding. It is interesting to look at how feeding develops, and to see how speech develops at the same time.

The only food a baby needs is milk, so the first movements made by his articulators are those he needs for sucking. His sucking is different from an adult's, as he uses his tongue rather than his lips, and presses it up against his palate. His first sounds, therefore, are very simple and consist mainly of cooing noises made as his tongue makes the only movements it has learned. When his tongue is at rest in his mouth, the back of it may touch his palate, so he will produce some 'back' sounds, such as [k] and [g]. During crying, he will be beginning to practise sounds which will later become vowels. When he begins to eat solid food, from three months onwards, he increases the use of his cheek muscles, which he has already exercised to some extent when gripping tight to the breast or bottle. He also learns to close his lips so that the food does not fall out again, which takes a while to learn and accounts for some of the general messiness of feeding a baby of this age, and he begins to use the tip of his tongue to move the food around. His speech begins to change and he begins to babble, using most of the sounds he will later use in speech, plus others which he will not need.

When he is around seven months old, he will begin to chew, and this will lead to an increase in the number of sounds he uses as his lips, tongue and soft palate become very efficient and well synchronised. He will also be showing interest in what is going on in his mouth and will often have his fingers or thumbs in there, which will give him an extra awareness of the movements he can make. Of course, the kinds of movements made during speech do not remain exactly the same as those used in feeding, but they increase in subtlety as he matures and as he practises sounds, so that he will eventually be able to put complicated strings of sounds together. His first words, however, will consist of simple sounds, strung together fairly inaccurately. He may say 'da-da', or 'ma-ma', or something else altogether, but whatever it may be, it represents a coming together of his language learning and his sound practice, and it is a pretty remarkable achievement, of which his parents will be justly proud.

So, if feeding is of importance to a child's articulation development, it is wise for a parent to pay some attention to his skill with feeding, for children vary in this as in everything else. In particular, when your child is beginning to eat 'adult' food and is chewing, try to vary the types and textures of foods, so that he can have as much exercise as possible for his articulatory muscles. As soon as he can manage solid pieces of food and does not choke too easily, offer him pieces of carrot and apple to chew rather than rusks and biscuits. This has of course the added benefit of being good for his diet and his teeth, so you can kill three birds with one stone! If you feel that your child is finding feeding very difficult and remains unable to chew his food long after his peers are well into mixed feeding, do have a word with your health visitor, who will be able to advise you on how to help him.

Finally, remember that your child will be listening to what you say and how you say it, and will be learning more from you than from anyone around him. So try to give him a good model, not by trying to talk in an unnatural exaggerated way or by trying to get rid of any accent you may have, but by talking calmly and reasonably slowly to him, by looking at him when you talk and by letting him look at you so that he can see what you are doing to make the sounds. Show him that making noises is fun by using the sounds that imitate real noises, such as 'splash' or car noises. And do remember to be positive and not to be critical of his attempts at speech, for there is a lot for him to learn!

How can sounds be grouped together?

There are fewer than 40 basic sounds in English, which are put together to make up thousands of different words. There is a list of the commonly used consonants in figure 2. It is very important that a child learns to make each of the sounds correctly, so that it is different from any other sound. This seems obvious,

Figure 2

Some of the consonants used in English

Sound	As used in
p	pie
b	by
m	my
t	toe
d	dough
n	no
k	key
g	go
ŋ	ring
f	foe
v	van
s	sue
z	zoo
ʃ	shy
ʧ	chew
θ	thin
ð	the
l	lie
r	row

but in fact some sounds can be very like others, with just one feature of difference. For example, the sound [t] is very like [d] in several ways. The tongue tip is raised to the ridge just behind the top teeth, which is called the alveolar ridge, and is held there while breath pressure builds up in the mouth. The soft palate is raised to form a seal with the back of the throat, to prevent air from escaping down the nose. After a moment, for both sounds, the tongue tip drops and the air is released with a small explosion. However, the difference between the two sounds is that no voice is used in [t], while the vocal cords in the voice

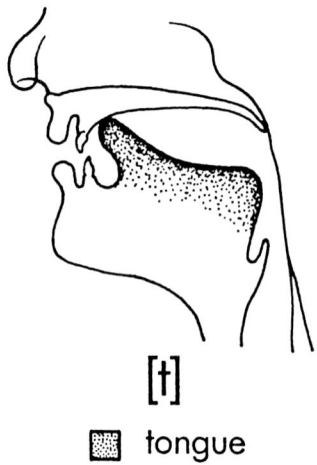

[t]

▓ tongue

To make the sound [t], the tongue tip is raised to touch the alveolar ridge

box vibrate together to give voice to [d]. I will be talking more about the vocal cords later.

There is also slightly greater force used to say [t] than is used for [d]. That is why you can still make the sounds seem different when you are whispering (that is, not using your voice at all). So it is possible to define the main features which are used in various combinations to give different sounds.

Firstly, there is the place of articulation, which is the part of the mouth where the sound is made. This may be the lips, in the case of [p] and [b], or the alveolar ridge in [t] and [z] and several other sounds. These are sometimes called the 'front' sounds. Or the back of the tongue may touch the back of the soft palate for the 'velar' or 'back' sounds [k] and [g].

Sounds can also differ according to whether the breath continues during the sound, as it does in [s] and [m], or whether it is stopped and then released suddenly as in [t] and [b]. If the breath continues, it may pass unimpeded in some sounds, such as [n], while in other sounds, such as [f] and [s], there is a certain amount of friction as the air passes along a very narrow channel made by the articulators.

Finally, there is the difference between sounds where the air passes through the mouth, as in [p], [l], or [g], and those where it passes down the nose, as in [m], [n], and [ŋ] which is the sound at the end of 'ring' and 'sang'. There are many other tiny differences between sounds which an expert in phonetics would recognise, but these are the main ways we can group sounds together when considering what our children are trying to learn. If you want to help your child's speech, it is much better to play games which will improve certain features of sounds,

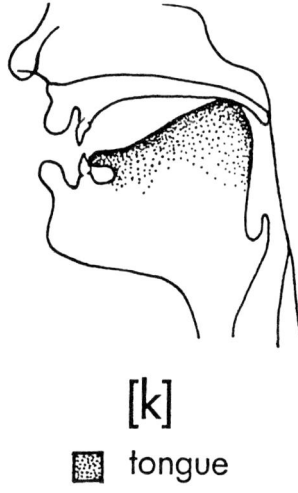

[k]

▦ tongue

To make the sound [k], the back of the tongue is raised to touch the soft palate

than to try to teach him individual sounds. There are games in the games chapter which will help him to listen to and recognise these features, without his needing to attempt sounds which he might find difficult. If you think your child's speech is more difficult to understand than it should be at his age, even taking

35

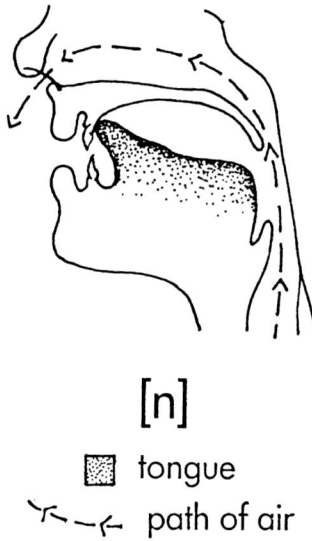

[n]

▦ tongue

ᔓ –ᔕ path of air

To make the sound [n], the soft palate is lowered to allow air to escape through the nose

into account the huge range of what is 'normal', then please get in touch with a speech therapist, who can tell you exactly which exercises will help your child. The games in this book are intended to improve children's speech, but obviously cannot be tailored to the particular needs of any one child, so should not be used to attempt to remedy things that might have gone wrong.

Why are some sounds so difficult?
There are some sounds which cause more worry for parents than others, and it is a good idea to think about some of these, and consider what makes them difficult for a child to learn.

The fricative sounds, which are those in which the breath

continues throughout the sound but is made to pass through a very small space so that there is a 'hissing' quality, often cause a little difficulty. This group includes [f], [s], [ʃ] (or 'sh'), [z] and [v]. These sounds are, for one thing, difficult to hear. They are the high-pitched sounds that become distorted on the telephone or on a tape recorder, and are the ones that we find it more difficult to hear if a cold is depressing our hearing. The slightest hearing loss tends to affect our discrimination of these sounds. This all means that a child needs to have very good hearing and also very good listening abilities before he can sort out what he is aiming to reproduce when he is saying these sounds. This is the first difficulty.

However, even if your child's listening skills are marvellous, these sounds remain a difficult group because they require an even finer control of the articulators than do other sounds. To take the [s] sound, for example, which is the sound over which parents most often feel concern. For this, the tongue tip is raised to the alveolar ridge, just behind the front teeth. But, instead of the tip touching the ridge, it is dropped slightly so that there is a small channel along the centre of the tongue. The breath will pass along this channel, which must be of exactly the right size to produce the characteristic 'hiss'. The sides of the tongue, meanwhile, must be pressed firmly up against the side teeth. If this seal is not complete, all sorts of peculiar variations on the [s] will be heard. It is hardly surprising if a child who is just learning to talk fails to get all these tiny movements exactly right to begin with.

Finally, these sounds are very important in contributing to the intelligibility of speech, and if they are not present, or are there in an incorrect form, it is immediately apparent to the listener that something is wrong with the speech. It also makes speech very difficult to understand if these sounds are missing, which explains why parents often feel very anxious. When these sounds appear, a dramatic improvement in a child's speech occurs, as it suddenly becomes much more intelligible. So do

37

not be too despondent if your two- or three-year-old uses speech which nobody apart from his immediate family can understand. These difficult sounds need to be given plenty of time to develop.

Even if a child is using all the sounds he needs in his speech, he can often experience difficulty in words where little clusters of consonants are grouped together. On the whole, vowels, which are the long-drawn-out, middle bits of words, are easier for a child to learn as they do not require complicated lip or tongue movements. Words which have many consonants and few vowels are naturally more difficult to say. These words have 'clusters' of consonants, and it requires a good deal of practice before a child can be guaranteed to move his articulators quickly and accurately enough to get these right. Words that give trouble can contain consonant clusters such as [pl] as in 'play', or [kr] as in 'cry'. If the cluster also contains one of the fricatives, any child will have difficulty. So words like 'exclaim' or 'flower' or 'spring' or 'squirrel' are some of the last words that you can expect your child to achieve. It is quite common for children starting school to stumble a little over these words, though they can probably make each of the sounds correctly when it is not surrounded by other consonants.

When you consider the problems encountered in learning sounds and how to put them together, it becomes much easier to accept the inevitable mistakes that your child makes as part of the learning process. Try not to expect his speech to be clear right from the beginning, and remember that the better his language, the more words he will be trying to say, so the more mistakes he will make. If, taking all this into account, you are still worried about his speech, then see a speech therapist now! So many parents worry for months before asking a speech therapist to see their child, when all therapists agree that they like to see a child as soon as his parents feel worried, if only to put the parents' minds at rest.

3
Voice

What is voice?

In the chapter on speech sounds, I mentioned the difference between voiced and unvoiced sounds. At this point it would be interesting and helpful to consider just what happens when we use our voices, since it involves yet more muscles and cartilages. There are several sounds which can be paired together because they are alike in all respects except for the question of whether or not voice is used to make them. For example, [t] and [d], [s] and [z], [p] and [b]. The first sound in each pair is described as voiceless, because it uses only breath to achieve it, and it has a characteristic 'hissing' quality. The second, or voiced, sound in each pair, however, has a 'buzzing' sound to it. This is the effect of the breath passing over the vocal cords whilst they are held close to each other, so that the breath makes them vibrate. This is what happens in the 'voice box' or larynx when we are talking.

The larynx is the hard 'Adam's apple' which is found in the neck, just below the chin. It is present in everyone, although it tends to be bigger and more noticeable in men. It is a hard structure, made of cartilage. (Cartilage is the material found at the end of the nose, and is more flexible than bone.) Inside the box are two cords which look more like lips than cords, and which run from front to back. These are the vocal cords. They remain open most of the time so that the breath can pass between them without making a noise, but they can be held together to vibrate or pushed tightly together to stop any breath escaping. They do this as we cough, and then move apart suddenly. This violent movement is designed to dislodge anything that may be between the cords which would prevent breathing. The length of the vocal cords determines whether the resulting voice is high or low, which is why a man's cords are larger and his 'Adam's apple' is bigger. The cords are capable of minute movements to increase or decrease their length, so that we are able to vary the pitch of our speech, or sing a tune.

The movement of the cords does not produce voice by itself, for there must be a steady stream of air passing between them. This air vibrates as it squeezes past the cords which have moved very close together, and it is this vibration that we hear as voice. So before good voice can be achieved, good breathing patterns are necessary. The breath, of course, comes from the lungs which are to be found in the chest. They are a pair of roughly triangular bags with the smallest part at the top. This means that most air comes from the bottom of the lungs, so people who breathe 'shallowly' and rapidly are only using a part of their lungs. They put in a good deal more hard work than they need to, and do not produce as strong and steady a voice as they should.

Children tend to be naturally good breathers at first and use most of their lungs, but it is as we get older that we begin to breathe shallowly, often moving our shoulders instead of inflating our lower chests. The better the breathing patterns, the better the voice that is achieved. This is why singers pay so much attention to their breathing, making sure they use their diaphragm. This is the muscle which stretches from front to back just below the lungs, dividing them from the rest of the body, and it pushes the air from the base of the lungs. There are some ideas in the games chapter of ways to improve a child's breathing patterns which will stand him in good stead for the rest of his life.

Once the breath is moving nicely over the vocal cords and they are vibrating properly, a small sound is produced which needs to get louder if it is to be heard. This happens when the vibrating air passes through the resonators. These are spaces inside the head where the air bounces around and vibrates more and more. They are called the sinuses and are usually empty, but when you have a cold, they become full of mucus, so that there is no room for the air to move and the voice is consequently muffled in quality. At the same time, the nose becomes blocked so that air cannot pass down for the nasal sounds [m] and [n]. If your child constantly sounds as though he has a cold, even when he does not have one, it may be that his adenoids and tonsils are enlarged.

The tonsils are at the back of the mouth, situated on either side, and they can be quite large and obvious in children without causing any problems. The adenoids are further back, out of sight, and if they become too large they may block off the air flow from the lungs to the nose, which gives the characteristic sound to the child's speech of a constant cold. The tonsils and adenoids do serve a useful purpose in helping the body's defences against infections, so doctors prefer not to remove them unnecessarily. Ask your doctor's advice if you are worried about your child's tonsils and adenoids.

4
Stuttering

How do you know if your child is stuttering?
There are many myths and half-truths spoken about stuttering, many of which fall into the 'old wives' tales' category. In this chapter I shall try to dispel a few of these. The first is the imagined difference between 'stammering' and 'stuttering'. There is in fact no difference at all, just a difference in terminology. This has developed over the years because research programmes have been underway both in the UK, where researchers have tended to talk about 'stammering', and in the USA, where they have used the word 'stuttering'. Nowadays, most of the people involved in research into the problem use the American term, so that is what I shall use in this chapter.

In general, people can tell when someone is stuttering. It is usually taken to be repetitions of sounds, often at the beginnings of words, and this is indeed one of the ways in which people stutter. When we think of a 'stutterer' we think of someone who says, 'M-M-My n-n-ame is J-J-J-John.' There are, however, many other ways in which people stutter. They may repeat a whole word, or a syllable of a word, so that they could say, 'My name is-is-is John' or 'I live in Man-Man-Manchester.' They may even block completely, so that no words come out at all, or they may choose to avoid a word that they believe they will be unable to say and use another word instead. Some stutterers are so good at changing their words if they think they are going to have difficulty that people listening to them are unaware that they have a speech problem at all.

In addition to the stuttering that can be *heard*, the person involved may have little grimaces or movements which he uses to help him to get started on what he is trying to say. Another habit is to lose eye-contact with the listener, by looking away, at anything except the listener's face.

With all these manifestations, it is clearly no joke at all to be a stutterer, even if your stutter is so unnoticeable that only you know that you have difficulty. Similarly, it is very distressing indeed for parents to see signs in their child that he is having difficulty in 'getting his words out.' They of course want to know whether this state of affairs is only temporary, or whether it will persist.

Research into the topic of stuttering is continuing vigorously at the moment, both in the UK and elsewhere and this book is not the place to discuss the various theories and their implications. However, I think it is helpful for parents who are concerned for their children to understand a little more about what the problem entails.

First of all, remember that many children go through a stage, as they are beginning to use better and richer language, when their speech is full of hesitancies and repetitions, and many parents feel that this is the beginning of stuttering. However, the child may well pass on from this stage and lose all the stuttering behaviour without ever being aware that there was anything the matter. This is called normal non-fluency (fluency being the normal flow of speech that we all expect to achieve). Children between two and five years of age can drift in and out of this state several times and they are not stutterers. If your child comes into this category, he will not be upset or embarrassed by his speech and will not look strained and panicky when he is talking. The non-fluency should remain something that only adults notice. Try to accept this as being a passing phase, albeit an irritating one, and your child will recover from it in time.

There are, however, some children who are unfortunate enough to go on to stuttering. This is not their fault, and it is important to remember that it is not the fault of their parents either. What causes stuttering in the first place remains a difficult and shadowy area. It is generally agreed that there are many factors which cause a predisposition, perhaps inherited, to turn into a stutter. These may include ill health, tiredness, stress or worry about speech itself. However, why one person stutters and another does not is still not known. Certainly, many researchers believe that a stutterer has a physical problem with co-ordinating all the movements required for speech. This is a relief to many parents, who may have been made to feel in the past that they are responsible for their child's difficulties. This is not the case, although there may be things a parent can do to help his dysfluent child. I shall talk about a few of these in this chapter. It is sometimes helpful for a parent to liken the tendency to stutter to the way that many people have a 'weak spot', perhaps a throat or back, where problems crop up from time to time according to outside circumstances. Viewed in this rather unscientific way it is easier to see why stuttering varies in intensity and frequency from person to person and even in the same person at different times.

If you are concerned that your child may be beginning to stutter, ask yourself the following questions. Does he worry about his speech? Has he said anything about it to you, or mentioned any other child's speech as being better than his? Does he avoid talking on occasions when he would previously have chattered happily? Does he look away from you when he starts to hesitate or repeat? Does he have twitches or grimaces which accompany his speech? Has he been talking like this for what you would consider a long time, for example, several months? If the answers to all these questions are no, then you need take no further action unless the situation changes and you feel he is beginning to feel unhappy. If you answer yes to some of the questions, your child may still be going through a normal stage of non-fluency, but either he or you are becoming very anxious about his speech and you should seek help from a speech therapist. Do not wait and worry, hoping that things will put themselves right. They may do so, but a chat with a therapist will help.

Is there anything you can do to help?

The short answer to this question is yes, you can help your child. The difficult part is in deciding how, because stuttering varies so very much between different people that there are a number of ways in which you could help, and each child can benefit from a different combination of ways of handling the problem. The best way to find out what you can do is to see your therapist, but it sometimes happens that there is a long waiting list for speech therapy, and of course you want to help right away. Here are a few suggestions for things you could think about before you and your therapist can work out a treatment. They may make life easier for your child while he is stuttering.

First of all, avoid saddling your child with the label of 'stutterer'. Don't say, in a cross voice, 'Stop stuttering and say it properly.' You may think you would never dream of being so tactless, but when your child is trying to tell you something, is unable to get the words out and you are rushing to get the dinner on the table, the whole situation can become very fraught. Try to keep calm. If you do not have time to stop and listen, then tell him to wait a minute, finish what you are doing and then give him your attention. There is no need to give him extra attention beyond that offered to other members of the family. The fact that you are worried about his speech is no reason to treat him with kid gloves or give him your undivided attention every time he opens his mouth.

On the other hand, let him have a fair crack of the whip in family conversations. It may be that more fluent brothers and sisters interrupt him, or talk over him, and if this is the case you will need to use tact and discretion. It is not helpful to tell the others to 'Let James talk' simply because he is the one with the

45

speech difficulty. This makes him stand out as different from the others. It would be better to have an agreement to take turns in talking, for example at the dinner table, so that James has a right to be heard, and also must stop and let someone else talk when he has had a turn. This may sound rigid and unnatural, but children take readily to this kind of rule. In fact, most households could benefit from this kind of agreement, as it lessens the general noise level!

Think a little about how you talk to your child. Do you tend to talk quickly, or slowly? Is your own speech smooth or jerky? Try to use the kind of quiet, smooth speech that you want your child to imitate when you speak to him. Avoid throwing sudden questions at him that need rapid replies, as he may find this an added stress if his speech is hesitant. Of course, do not use a noticeably different way of talking to him from that which you use with the rest of the family. You may well find that using slightly slower speech to everyone and trying to talk calmly has a beneficial effect on the whole family.

When your child is talking to you, listen to what he is saying, rather than concentrating on the way he is talking. This is how you listen to other speakers. If you are waiting for hesitations you are very likely to give a slight indication by your expression, which your child will notice, whenever one occurs. If you are determined to concentrate on what he is talking about, you will avoid generating this kind of tension.

Consider how your day is divided up. Do you have time alone with each child? For many of us, this is very difficult to arrange, but it usually repays the effort you have to make. Spend a short time, even if it is only a quarter of an hour, alone with your child, and during this time play a game with him, or read to him, or get him to help you to set the table for dinner, or do some gardening together. The important thing is that you spend the time happily together, not worrying about speech, just showing your child that you enjoy his company. When you do this, remember to set aside time for any other children in just the same way. Never treat the dysfluent member of the family as though he is 'special' because of his speech. This is easier said than done, because to watch your child struggling to talk makes you want to 'make it up to him' in other ways, but this would not help him in the long run to talk better.

Think positively about his speech. Notice how often he talks without hesitating. He may sing or talk to the family dog, or to one parent, sibling or friend perfectly fluently. This does not mean that he is 'putting it on' when he is dysfluent, but it does mean that he is capable of fluent speech on at least some occasions, so there is something for him to build on.

Do remember, however, that these suggestions are intended only to take a little of the strain off your child while he is having difficulties. Do not try to use them instead of seeing a speech therapist, who will be able to give you advice and help tailored to your child. Different and better ways of treating stuttering are being developed all the time, and the whole problem is of great current interest to speech therapists.

5
Games

The games in this chapter are grouped according to the skills that they are designed to improve, the parts of speech that they teach and the types of sounds that they practise. Before playing these games with your child, it is most important that you have read the chapters on Language and Speech Sounds, so that you are quite sure what you are trying to achieve with each game.

Once you have decided that you are ready to play, choose very carefully which games you play and when. Some will involve your child in a vigorous activity, such as running around the room, whilst others will need a high degree of concentration and will require him to sit still for a few minutes. It is as well to alternate these different kinds of activity in order to keep him interested and to avoid labouring one point too much. Keep the games short and always finish before your child becomes bored, even if this means only two minutes of a particular activity. Once a child has lost interest you are wasting your time trying to continue, and you will simply feel angry with him. Always remember that the onus is on you to keep him interested, and if he is not enjoying a game or is finding it too difficult, it is because you have pitched it at the wrong level.

Although you will be aware that the games you are playing are intended to improve your child's speech, there is no reason why he should know that. So far as your child is concerned, the games are just good fun. Do not draw too much attention to his speech when you are playing, and certainly avoid asking him to repeat words or 'say it properly'. Remember the sequence of language learning: understanding comes well before expression.

Always keep your sessions of play short, and try to move smoothly from one game to another. Five or ten minutes of games every day will show much quicker results than half an hour once a week and will keep your child wanting more. However, if he does not seem in the mood one day or if you feel too rushed or irritable yourself, give the games a miss. Try them another day when you are both in the mood.

Some games here will call for 'picture cards'. Make these by cutting out small cards, at least three inches square, and either draw the appropriate picture or cut it out of a magazine and stick it on. Make sure that your preparation is all completed before you embark on a game so that you do not have to stop and search for equipment while you are playing.

GAMES TO DEVELOP LANGUAGE SKILLS

Attention and listening

It is vital that your child should be able to control his own attention and is not so easily distracted by everything around him that he cannot listen to what people are saying to him. You can begin to train a baby's attention from a very early age. In fact, you probably do it without realising what you are doing when you play 'Peep-bo' with your child, for this game encourages him to keep looking for your face even when you have hidden it from him for a few seconds. The enormous reward he receives when your face reappears encourages him to play the game again, and each time he plays he is improving his ability to focus his attention.

When you play one of the attention games listed here, make it as easy as possible for your child to concentrate. Sit him down in a comfortable chair, at a table, and sit opposite him. Make sure there are no obvious distractions, such as someone mowing the lawn outside and passing the window every few minutes, or a radio playing. Try to choose a time when no one is likely to burst into the room and make sure the child does not desperately need a drink, something to eat or a visit to the toilet. Have any equipment necessary for the game ready at hand and then begin. If your child is a real fidget, do not be afraid to hold his hands (gently) with yours, and make sure he is looking at you when you speak. Eye-contact is vitally important for helping him to listen.

Jack-in-the-box

This is a very simple game that you can play with a young baby or toddler. Use an ordinary jack-in-the-box and play with it as normal for a few minutes to establish that your child understands how to make the puppet jump up. Then introduce a variation. Hold your child's hands, call his name so that he looks at you, then say 'Go' and release his hands so that he presses the button to make the puppet jump up. If he does not press it straight away, do this yourself, so that it happens as soon as you have given the signal. Do this two or three times so that your child understands the idea, then reverse things so he has a chance to shout 'Go'. Even a young baby who is not talking will produce some sort of sound as the signal. As you play the game over a period of days, you can lengthen the time he has to wait for the signal, and thus increase the time he has to listen and concentrate.

Instruments

Older pre-school children enjoy this game. You will need two each of a selection of simple instruments or noise-makers such as rattles, squeaky toys, bells or yoghurt pots filled with different, noisy things such as dry spaghetti, peas, sugar or sand, and covered well with cling-film so that your child cannot eat the contents. Make sure they are matching pairs, so that each one

'Jack-in-the-box': Training your child to listen for a signal

1 Listening
2 Carrying out an action on hearing a signal
3 That was fun!

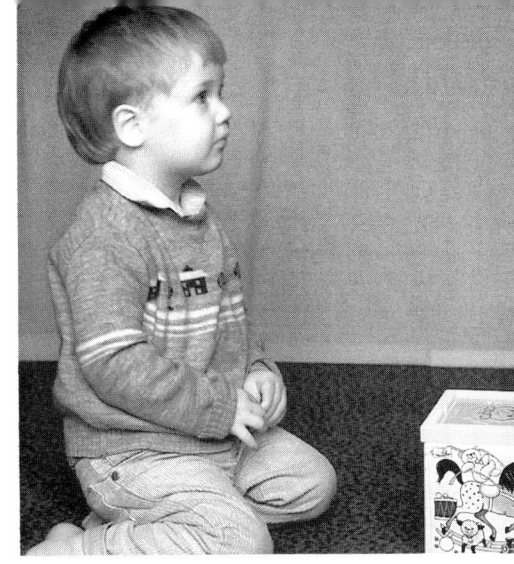

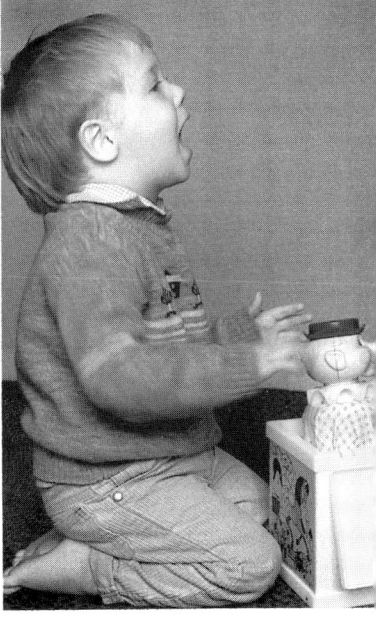

of a pair both looks and sounds like the other.

Put two different instruments on the table in front of your child. For example, a rattle and a bell. Let him play with them to hear the noises they make and show him that you have the other halves of the pairs. Then hide your instruments under the table and make a noise with one of them. See if he can pick out his corresponding instrument and repeat the noise. Then bring out the instrument you used to show him that he was right.

You can make this game more and more complicated as he becomes skilful by introducing pairs of sound makers which are close in sound to others. Your yoghurt-pot shakers are a good way to do this. Make sure that you paint the outsides of the shakers in paired colours, so that you do not have to spend hours sorting out the pairs before each game!

Sound lotto
You will need plenty of time to prepare the equipment for this game, but it is well worth the time spent as children always enjoy it. You will need a tape recorder, picture cards and some counters.

Record some everyday sounds on your tape recorder. For example, a bird, a car, a tap dripping, a television, children playing, a man talking, someone singing. Use some sounds that are of particular interest to your child, such as the noise made by his own drum or trumpet, or the family cat. Leave a gap of a few seconds between each sound. Make up a picture card to illustrate each sound.

You are now ready to play the game. Put three of the cards in front of your child, and give him a handful of counters. Say 'Listen', make sure he is looking at you, then play one of the sounds on the tape recorder and let your child put a counter on the corresponding picture. If he finds it very easy, put more of his cards out at the same time so that he has to find the picture from amongst several others. Sometimes make him listen to more than one of the sounds before putting the counters on, so that he is improving his memory at the same time. You will have to put in a little practice with your tape recorder so that you can go fairly quickly from one sound to another without always playing the sounds in the same order.

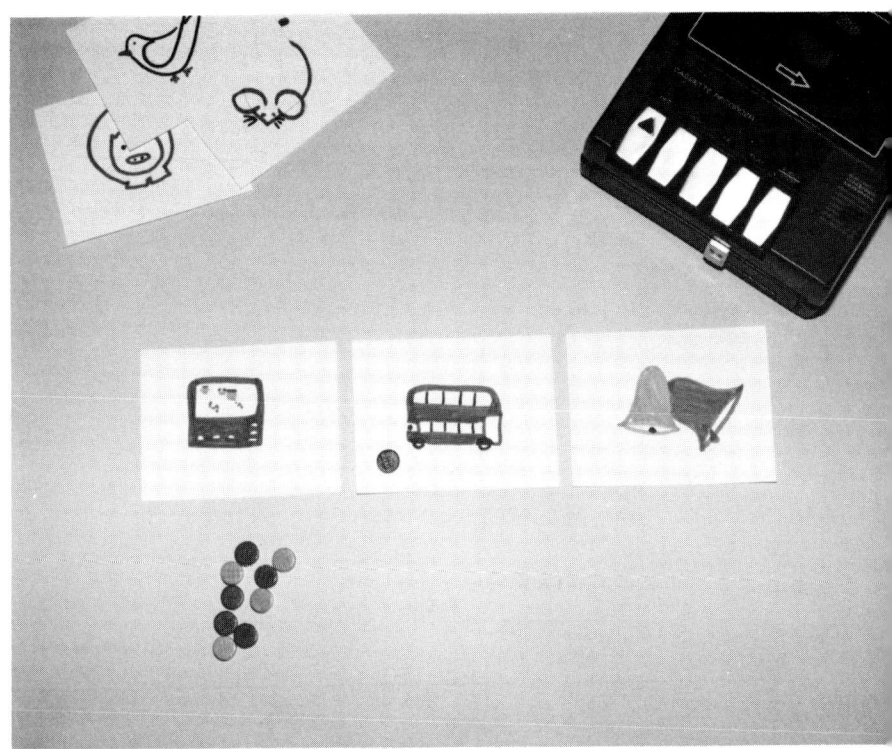

'Sound lotto': listening for everyday sounds

Sound chart

Use a large sheet of paper divided into seven sections, one for each day of the week. Have ready some sticky stars.

Every day choose one sound, such as a dog barking or an aeroplane. Choose something that your child is likely to hear several times in one day. Draw or stick on a picture of the chosen sound in the section for that day and tell your child to listen out for that sound during the day. Every time he hears the sound he is allowed to stick on a star.

A variation on this game, to play with an older child, is to use a different word for each day, or even a different speech sound.

Monday — car

Tuesday — laughing

Wednesday — dog

Thursday — cows

Friday — singing

Saturday — piano

Sunday — baby

'Sound chart'

Story

Read or tell your child a story, telling him beforehand that he must listen out for a certain word. Every time he hears that word he is to perform an agreed action. He could, for example, jump up in the air every time he hears the word 'up' (see sample story), or clap every time he heard the word 'the'. You could ask an older child to listen out for one speech sound, such as [p] or [s]. When you play this game, make sure that your child returns to a quiet, listening position, preferably sitting down, in between the actions. It can be helpful if another adult is there to help the child to sit quietly.

'Story': listening out for certain words in a story

Incidentally, if you are using a story from a book be sure that you know how often the chosen word is going to occur, as any child will become frustrated if he only hears his word once. Older children or those who are becoming good at listening might like to listen out for two or three words at the same time.

Sample story:　　Teddy gets **up** to mischief

One night, a naughty teddy bear was asleep in bed with his owner, Christopher. Suddenly, he woke **up**. He looked around, but Christopher was fast asleep, so Teddy thought he would get **up** to some mischief by himself.

He jumped out of bed, and set off down the ladder from the bunk. He noticed he was not wearing his bow-tie and as he always liked to be smartly dressed he climbed **up** the ladder again. He found his tie and tried to tie it, but he got in a real muddle. 'Oh dear, I always mess this **up**' he said.

He set off down the ladder again, slipped on the end of his tie and tumbled head first to the floor. He had a nasty bump on his nose, but Teddy was much too brave to cry, so he just picked himself **up** and set off again.

Very quietly, he crept out of the door and down the stairs to the kitchen. Christopher's mummy and daddy were asleep **up**stairs, so it was very quiet and dark. Teddy tiptoed over to the fridge, opened the door, and had a look inside. Oh yes, there was a bottle of milk. He would make **up** a milk shake. He found the powder, put it in a cup with the milk and gave it a good shake. The cup shot **up** in the air and fell to the floor, spilling milk shake everywhere.

'Oh dear,' said Teddy. 'I'd better clean it **up**.' He grabbed a cloth and started to mop the floor. Unfortunately, a box of cornflakes was sitting on the table and he bumped it with his elbow. The box tipped **up** and the cornflakes fell into the puddle of milk. Teddy could hardly believe his eyes. He grabbed a dustpan and brush, swept the whole mess **up** and put it in the dustbin. Then he ran **up**stairs as fast as he could and jumped back into bed.

Next morning, Christopher and his mummy could not understand why an empty milk bottle was **up** in the cornflakes cupboard, while the cornflakes were in the fridge. Teddy has been in such a hurry that he had mixed them **up**. He decided never to get **up** to mischief again, and he didn't – until the next time!

Pairs of words

There are many words which sound almost the same as each other, but which contain one sound which makes them different, as in 'cat' and 'hat'. These are sometimes called 'Minimal pairs'. There is a list of some of these in figure 3.

Make up some picture cards to illustrate these words. Put two of the cards on the table in front of your child, then hold a piece of paper over your mouth so that he cannot see your lips move. Remember to keep your eyes uncovered so that you can maintain eye-contact. Say one of the words, quite quietly, and let your child pick up the one you say. See how quietly you can whisper the words whilst still getting the right response from your child.

Figure 3

Minimal pairs

The words in these groups sound the same as each other in all respects except one.

cat hat mat fat	tin bin thin pin	mac mat man	bike bite	like light
boot hoot shoot	sing thing ring	boy toy	bill till fill hill mill	mouth mouse
hot cot	car bar	bull full	well bell	

Sequencing and memory

In order to express himself well, a child must be capable of remembering a series of words. First of all he must be able to remember the words he hears long enough to work out their meaning, and secondly he must be able to put together a meaningful sentence or phrase without forgetting what he was saying

'Farm animals': a simple memory game

before he reaches the end. Similarly, he needs to be able to remember a sequence of sounds correctly so that he can put them together himself in the form of words. Children who have poor phonology are often found to have a poor auditory memory. This is a skill which is amenable to improvement with practice, so the following games should be of benefit to any child.

Farm animals
Use a set of ordinary farm animals. Show them one at a time to your child and name them. Make sure that he knows their names well by asking him to 'show me the cow', 'show me the sheep' and so on. Also make sure he knows the words 'field',

'barn', 'fence' or any other items you are using. There is no need for him to be able to say the words, just understand them.

Now begin to give him very simple instructions, such as 'Put the pig in the field.' (He does not need to understand the word 'in' to follow this instruction, just 'pig' and 'field'.) Then say 'Put the pig and the cow in the field', and if he can manage these two items, say 'Put the pig, cow and sheep in the field.' When he begins to make mistakes, you will know that you have asked for too many items at a time, so go back a step. Keep the game light, so that your child never feels that he is being tested, or that it matters if he forgets something. Turn the game round so that he has a turn at giving you instructions, even if these consist of only one word. This will give him a fine experience of using language in a pleasant way.

Dressing up

This is an active game which can be great fun after a more concentrated game such as one from the Attention and Listening section. You will need a pile of dressing-up clothes with as many different kinds of garments as possible, including gloves, hats, scarves, jumpers, pyjamas and so on. You will also need a kitchen timer or a watch with an alarm.

Put the pile of clothes at one end of the room, stand at the other end with your child and say, 'Before the bell rings you must put on a hat and a cardigan.' Then set the timer or watch for a reasonable length of time, depending on how quickly your child can get himself dressed. Most children will need about two minutes if they are playing a game, in spite of the fact that they would take ten if they were dressing in the morning! If the bell rings before your child is dressed or if he forgets an item, make him pay a forfeit such as turning a somersault or hopping across the room. Then let him give the instruction to you, and you do the dressing up.

Remember that the point of the game is to improve his memory, so gradually increase the number of items he has to

put on, and ensure that he puts them on in the correct order.

I went to market
This is a variation on the well-known game.

Make up picture cards of things that you might buy in the shops. Anything will do, from a stripy sock to a bag of beans. Try to make the objects as interesting as possible, and enlist your child's help in making the cards.

Put them, face down, in a pile on the table. Pick up the top one and say, 'I went to the market and bought a big banana' (or whatever the card shows). Show the card to your child, then put it, face down, in front of him. He must then repeat, 'I went to the market and bought a big banana' (turning up the banana card) 'and' (taking the top card from the pile) 'a fat hen'. In this way you will build up a line of cards. Your child will remember the items more easily, and thus enjoy the game more, using picture cards, and turning the cards over each time will fix them better in his memory. It will also prevent arguments!

Frog story
Make up a story which includes a growing list of things. It is a good idea to use a puppet or a favourite toy as the hero of the story. Here is an example, using a toy frog.

Frog woke up one morning and remembered that this was the day that his Aunt Jemima was coming to tea. He would have to make plenty of cakes because he knew that there was nothing in the world she liked more than cakes for tea. He looked at his watch and saw that it was very late, so he set out straight away – without making a list!

He ran as fast as he could to the shops, then ran home again holding a large package. He got out his mixing bowl.

'Dressing up'

61

'Oh dear', he said. 'I've got the flour, but I forgot the chocolate. Aunty does like chocolate cake.' So he rushed off to the shops again.

When he got home, he put the shopping on the table. 'Oh dear,' he said. 'I've got the flour and the chocolate, but I forgot the butter. You can't make a proper cake without butter.' So he rushed off to the shops again.

Continue in this way, adding items to the list. Your child will join in the list as it gets longer. Finally, round off your story in an interesting way.

At last Frog, who was very hot and very tired by this time, had bought all the things he needed to make the cakes for Aunt Jemima. He had the flour, the chocolate, the butter, the eggs, the milk, the icing and the decoration to go on the top. He was very pleased with himself. Then he looked at the calendar and realised that Aunt Jemima wasn't coming today at all, but next week.

'Oh bother!' he said. 'I shall just have to eat the cakes myself.'

So that is what he did!

You will be able to think of many variations on this kind of story, such as Frog getting dressed in the morning, one piece of clothing at a time, or collecting musical instruments for a band's performance. Children become very involved in these stories, and will suggest more items for the lists.

Single nouns

The first words that your child is likely to say are nouns, or naming words. When he is just beginning to try out words, even if they sound very unlike the adult version, he will be interested in games that introduce him to new names. Do remember, however, the golden rule that understanding always comes before expression. Never expect your child to use words that he does not fully understand, and always play word games with him paying all your attention to his understanding and letting him say the words if and when he feels like it.

Everyday objects
Use the things that your child recognises as his own. Use his hairbrush, cup, plate, spoon, shoe, book. Make sure that you are using real things, not toys for this game. Put two or three objects out on the table in front of him, get his attention by

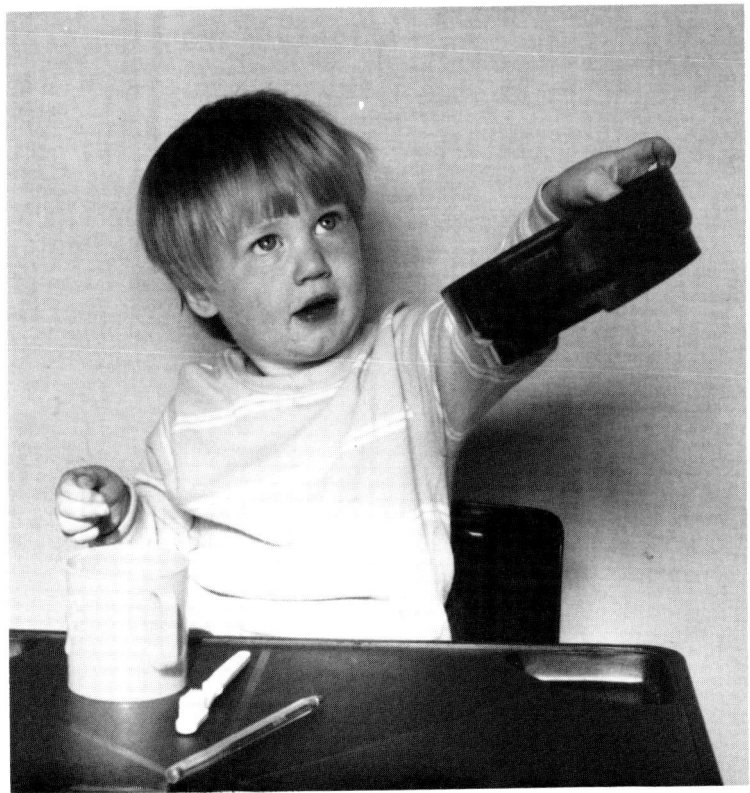

'*Everyday objects': choosing one item from several, in response to your instruction*

63

calling his name or gently touching him and say, 'Where's the book?' Keep looking him in the eye, and do not be tempted to glance at the object yourself as he will pick up this sort of clue. In response to the question, he may pick up or point to the object, or he may just look at it. This means that you must be very alert to notice what he does, so that you can praise him for 'eye-pointing' at the right object. If he is doing this, it is probably because he feels a little unsure of himself, and as he gets more confident, especially if you do not badger him to pick up the object, he will begin to respond in a more obvious way.

This simple game can be played with quite tiny children, so long as they are able to sit and attend for a few minutes. But do not expect them to go on for very long, as a child at this level of language learning will lose interest and needs to move on to a more active game quite quickly. Stop as soon as you feel his enthusiasm flagging. You can vary the game by finding pictures of the same objects and playing with these. If your child makes attempts to say the words as you are playing, be pleased and encouraging, but avoid making too much of a big deal out of it. The best attitude to have is that you knew he was a clever boy, and you are glad he is proving you right. This attitude will avoid too much effusiveness which can often make a child feel self-conscious.

Hidden objects
Use a bag which is big enough to hold some of your child's own objects. The ones you use for the 'Everyday objects' game (page 63) will do nicely. Put several objects in the bag, hold the bag up and say, 'What have I got in my bag today?' Put plenty of enthusiasm into your voice. Then make a big show of slowly bringing out the object, at the same time saying, 'Look, it's a . . .' and leave a pause as the object appears, in the hope that he will say the word. If he does not, you say it yourself, give him the object and let him play with it for a moment, before putting it out of sight and repeating the whole process with the next

object. This game needs great enthusiasm on your part, so that your child is filled with excitement as the object appears.

My book
Make a scrapbook of the things that are important to your child. Include photographs of members of the family and pets, magazine pictures of cups like his own or toys that he plays with. Make sure that every picture is of something he likes, even if you have to draw his teddy yourself. Put a photograph of him on the outside and write his name in large letters. Take every opportunity to sit down with him to look at the book together, and talk in simple sentences about the pictures. Make sure you use the name of the object each time. 'Oh, look, there's Granny. She's got her funny hat on' is a good length for him to take in. This book will probably be much loved and may become rather battered, but if your child wants to take it to bed with him, let him. Even a child who usually refuses to sit and look at books will be interested in one about himself.

You will find that once your child begins to use single words, his vocabulary will grow rapidly without your having to teach each new word. To help him to increase his vocabulary, share with him an interest in the things around him, pointing out and naming objects of interest such as aeroplanes and cars. Once he is using several different naming words, he will be ready to learn action words or verbs, so try a few of the verb games. Make sure you give him plenty of time to enjoy himself, and avoid trying to push him on too fast. Keep all the games light-hearted and fun.

Action words
Busy teddy
Use a teddy for this game if your child has one that he is fond of. Otherwise, use his favourite soft toy, although it helps the game along if you can use a toy with arms and legs. A cuddly

snake is rather lacking in possibilities for action games!

Tell your child that 'Teddy is a very busy teddy and he never sits still for a moment. Look what he can do.' Make teddy perform a simple action, such as walking. Say, 'He's walking.' Then show teddy doing one or two other actions, such as sitting, jumping, hopping, clapping or dancing. Then give teddy to your child and say, 'Make teddy jump,' and help him to make teddy do it. Only introduce one or two actions at a time, so that your child can easily remember them. Keep the game interesting by making teddy do funny things sometimes, such as tripping or sneezing, and keep your sentences short.

Yes–no game

Use your child's teddy again for this game, or vary it by using a different toy, or perhaps a puppet. You hold teddy and make him perform an action. Say, 'Is teddy jumping?' and then answer yourself: 'Yes, he's jumping.' Make teddy do another action and say again, 'Is teddy jumping?' Then shake your head vigorously and say, 'No, he isn't jumping, is he? He's eating!' Repeat the game, sometimes matching your words to the actions and sometimes getting it wrong. If you say the wrong word, make it very clear that it is wrong. Laugh about it with your child. Get him to indicate whether you are right or wrong, and let him grab teddy away from you to show you how to make him do the action that you said. Play this game strictly for laughs, and use words that he is already familiar with.

Scrapbook

Make a scrapbook containing pictures of people doing things. A few pieces of paper stapled together will do just as well as an expensive book from the shops, but use large pieces so that you can put several pictures on one page. Find, cut out and stick in pictures of actions, using one action per page. You might, for

'Busy teddy': making teddy sit is learning verbs the easy way

example, have a page full of people running, or of dogs barking. The most important part of the exercise is choosing the pictures with your child and deciding which page they go on. This will involve your child in decisions such as, 'Do you think this man is running or walking?' He may just answer by pointing to the appropriate page, but at least he is understanding and using the concept of running. Let him help with the sticking in, perhaps using the glue sticks that are available as these are less messy than flour and water.

As your child begins to use some action words as well as names of things, his language will increase by leaps and bounds, for by putting these words together he will be able to say many different things. He will begin to use little phrases and you can play games to encourage this.

Short phrases
Doll's tea party
To play this game, you will need to use at least two different types of toy, such as a doll and a teddy. You can of course substitute toy dogs, cats or rabbits, according to your child's preferences. You will also need toy cups, plates, spoons, knives and any other pretend 'tea' things.

The phrases you will be encouraging are those that use a name and action word together. For example, 'dolly drinking' (or sitting or cutting), or 'teddy eating' (or sleeping). Of course, your child will not say the words as beautifully as you do, and he is bound to leave off the 'ing ending. It does not matter at all at this stage.

Set out your tea party with your child, talking about all the items you are using to make sure that he knows all the words. Then get teddy, sit him on a chair and say, 'What's teddy doing?' If your child answers at all, say 'Yes, teddy's sitting.' Even if he does not answer, give the answer yourself. At this point you are providing him with a model so that he hears the

'Doll's tea party':   *'Look, monkey's drinking.'*

'Look, dolly's drinking.'

'What's happening?'

phrases you are teaching him. Then repeat the sequence using the doll. When you have done this, take both the teddy and the doll away, then put one back again. This time ask, 'What's happening?' In this way you encourage your child to put the two words together, to say, 'Teddy's sitting.'

Carry on with the tea party, using two-word phrases yourself whenever you can, and from time to time asking, 'What's happening?' The cunning part of the proceedings is using two characters, for if you only used the doll, your child would only have to give one word to answer the question. He could just say, 'Sitting'. As you play, let your child lead the game some-times. If he wants to give the toys a drink, then let him, but be on the alert for the two-word phrases you can use. Finish the

Let your child lead the game sometimes

game off by producing a real tea party for your child and yourself.

Activity race

This game is best played outside, and is fun if your child has a friend of about the same age as himself. However, he will still enjoy the activities by himself, especially if he is about two to three years old. The equipment you will need is simple. Use three or four items that you can do things with, such as a ball, rattle, cushion and stick. You will also need a whistle or noise maker of some kind to use as a starting signal.

Draw a line on the floor, or put down a marker, and stand the child behind it. A little way away, far enough so that he will have to run, line up your objects. Say, 'When I blow the whistle, go and kick the ball.' Then blow the whistle and let him go. Next time, give a different instruction such as 'Throw the cushion' or 'Shake the rattle.' Try to ask him to do something unexpected from time to time, such as 'Kick the stick' or 'Shake the ball.' This will keep him on his toes. You can turn the game around, and let him tell you what to do.

Indoor activities

For this less strenuous, indoor version of the activity race, you can use the furniture and surroundings in the room, such as chairs, the floor, cushions, a newspaper and perhaps any odd box that you happen to have lying around! Give your child instructions, saying what he must do, and with which item. He could sit on the box, hop on the newspaper or lie on the chair. Make sure that you tell him to do each action 'on' something, as to vary this with 'under', 'over' or 'in' would confuse the issue, but try to be as inventive as possible.

By the time your child has got to this stage in his language learning, he will be able to say many different things and will be becoming more confident. However, do not expect him to reach this stage as soon as you start playing language games with him. It can take many months for him to reach this level, and you will need to vary the games so that he continues to enjoy them. It is often fun for him to go back to the earlier games and play them again. This is a good idea if you feel he is not showing much progress, for you will notice how much more easily he copes with the instructions in the simpler games.

Remember also that his language will not develop steadily, but will improve in fits and starts. Each noticeable improvement will be followed by a time of consolidation, when it will be difficult for you to see an improvement. Nevertheless he will suddenly begin to show progress again, if you are patient.

The remaining language games will introduce wider concepts and more advanced parts of speech. There is no need to stick rigidly to the order in which they are described, because children vary in the order in which they learn new ideas, but by referring to the list of grammatical parts of speech in the Language chapter you will be able to tell which ones your child may be ready to learn. If you are not sure, then just play games that you think your child will enjoy.

Adjectives

Once a child is able to use adjectives to describe things, his language becomes richer and more exact. He will be able to tell you precisely what he means, and will get more fun out of talking. However, using adjectives is more than just remembering each word, for it involves the understanding of whole concepts such as colour, size or texture. This is what you will be teaching your child in these games. Once you have chosen a concept to work on, seize any opportunity to discuss it with your child. For example, if you are dealing with colours, point out things that have similar colours. You might point out that a bus is red, like his trousers, or that several of his toys are the same colour. Be prepared for arguments, as children will often refuse to accept that two shades of red can still be labelled red, and their observation can be very acute!

Colour boxes

Use three large boxes, and paint or cover them in different colours. The primary colours are good ones to begin with, so you might choose red, blue and green for your boxes. Ask your child to find objects with the colours on one of the boxes. Hold up a red brick and say, 'This brick is red. Can you find me another red brick?' If he brings one, let him put it in the red box, then let him find his own red objects.

When you have played this with each of the coloured boxes, on different occasions, you can bring out a whole armful of objects, and get him to put them one by one in the correct boxes. Remind him with each object of the name of the colour, and sometimes ask, 'What colour is this one?' As always, do not worry if he does not give you the answer each time, but if he says the wrong word correct him gently. Say, 'No, it's blue, and it goes in the blue box.' Make sure you always correct him, kindly, if he gets it wrong, because it will only confuse him if you allow him to call a red object green. Do not fall into the trap of being afraid to tell him when he is wrong, in the fear that you will stop him wanting to talk. If he is especially sensitive to his own mistakes, then only ask him questions when you know he will get the answer right. For example, you might show him a red brick, say, 'This is red,' and put it in the red box. Then pick up another one, exactly the same, and ask him the colour. He is pretty sure to get that one right!

Sizes
Many of the words that describe size have an opposite, and this is very useful when you are introducing these words to your child. When you talk about big, you can talk about small. You can contrast fat with thin, long with short, and wide with narrow.

Opposites wall chart
Divide a large sheet of paper into two columns and fix it on the wall. Choose a pair of opposites and label the columns. You might, for example, have columns labelled 'fat' and 'thin'. You and your child can then cut out or draw pictures of things that can go in the columns, but each picture must have an opposite. This can mean a great deal of searching through magazines, and can be quite difficult. If you have two or more children, make it a competition, as a five-year-old will enjoy it as much as a three-year-old. You may have to give a little more help to the younger child if you want to avoid too many quarrels! The finished charts will look good pinned up in their bedrooms.

Story
Make up a story in which you use many descriptions of size, with many of the 'size' adjectives followed by the opposite word. As you tell your story, let your child have the opportunity to choose some of the adjectives. Here is an example of the kind of story you might use.

Tony, the Magic Mouse

Tony was magic. He was a tiny mouse who lived in a small hole. He had a friend who was a huge elephant, living in an enormous house. Tony knew many magic spells, but his favourite was the one he called the 'Reversing Spell'. This spell made everything the opposite. Big things became small, fat things became thin, and hot things became cold.

One day, Tony was fed up. His friend Nora, the big elephant, had been teasing him because he was so small.

'Goodness me,' she said. 'You're so tiny that I nearly trod on you!'

Tony did not like being teased, and he decided to get his own back. He fetched his mirror, which he used for his spells, and he looked hard into it. 'Fiddle faddle, I don't give a fig. Make little things turn out big!' he whispered. Then he closed his eyes.

When he opened them again, he looked down, and was surprised to see that his feet, which were usually to be found near his chin, had almost disappeared from view, because instead of being a short mouse he was now very tall indeed. He gave a little skip of delight and looked around. Outside his hole, which had been so minute but which was now gigantic, he could see a small, thin elephant. Could this be his friend, the big, fat Nora? Tony giggled to himself. He went into his sitting room to sit on his favourite chair which was always nice and soft. But when he sat on it, it was too hard to be comfortable. He felt thirsty and went outside to have a drink from the river, but the water was no longer wet. It had become quite dry. Tony didn't like it at all. He thought he would have a cold ice cream instead, but when he took one out of the fridge it burnt his tongue because it was so hot.

Tony became more and more annoyed. 'It's all your fault,' he said to the tiny elephant. 'I've a good mind to tread on you!'

He marched towards Nora, looking so cross that she

began to cry. 'Please don't, she sobbed. 'I'm sorry I was unkind to you. I won't ever laugh at you again. Please make me huge again. I don't like being tiny.'

Tony picked up his mirror, which was difficult, because instead of being hard and firm, it had become soft and floppy. Still, he managed it, looked into it and winked three times. He closed his eyes, then opened them again. Everything was back to normal.

Tony began to laugh. 'I wouldn't have trodden on you,' he said. 'But it would have served you right.'

Nora picked up a trunkful of water and squirted it at her friend. 'At least the water is wet again,' she laughed.

Texture

There are many adjectives that deal with the texture or 'feel' of things, and you can play some interesting games to introduce these words to your child.

Feely box

Use a large cardboard box with a hole in one side big enough for your hand to go in. The box should also have a lid which you can fasten down. Collect together some articles which feel different from each other. You could use a cuddly toy (which is soft), a pencil (hard), a piece of knitting (woolly), some tree bark (rough), an apple (smooth), a brush (bristly).

Put the articles in the box, then put your hand in and get hold of one of them. Pull it out of the box, describing it on the way, and making sure you repeat the relevant adjective more than once. Your child might be able to guess what the object is, but in any case, pull it out and show it to him. Let him hold it and stroke it himself. Then let him feel in the box and try to describe the feel of the next object so that you can guess what it is. If he finds it difficult to think of the words at first, you could pull each one of the objects out yourself, describing them as you do so and then put them back and let him have a go once he has seen them.

Collage
Draw some outlines of objects on a large piece of paper, making them into a picture if you are sufficiently artistic, and fill in the outlines using materials which have the right 'feel'. For example, you could draw a rabbit, and fill it in with fur fabric, a mirror (tin foil), a table (wood), a frog (leather). If you do not trust your drawing talents too well, you could make a book out of thin card, and draw one outline on each page. Collage pictures are great fun, and your child will have many opportunities to discuss with you the best materials for each outline. Be prepared to go along with his suggestions, even if you do not entirely agree with them, so long as he can make a reasonable case for what he suggests. This means that he will really be using language in a constructive way, and also that he will feel the picture or book is truly 'his' work. Try to resist the temptation to do much of the sticking yourself. This is sometimes very difficult when you are watching your child stick things on slightly askew, but you have to grit your teeth and tell yourself that it is his picture, and if the rabbit's tail ends up half-way up the rabbit's back, that is the way it will have to be!

General adjective games
Tasting
Have ready a tray holding various food items which you have prepared. Try to make them as varied as possible in shape, size, texture and taste. Keep the tray covered so that your child cannot see the items before the game begins. Blindfold him, and put one of the pieces of food in his mouth. Try to avoid using things you know he hates, as he could well refuse to play any more and may never let you blindfold him again! Tell him to think of as many things as he can to say about the food before he tells you what it is. Help him by prompting him with suitable questions, such as 'Is it big or small? What shape is it? Is it sweet or sour?' Keep a score of the number of things he can say about each item, so that next time you play the game he can try to

beat his own record. He may want you to put the blindfold on and have a turn at guessing the food, but it is wise to be wary and if possible cheat a little by not having the blindfold on properly, so that you are not surprised by anything nasty arriving in your mouth!

Zoo animals
This game is a variation on the 'I went to market' game (page 61), but in this case you say, 'I went to the zoo and saw a hairy gorilla.' Your child then follows by saying, 'I went to the zoo and saw a hairy gorilla and a fat elephant.' Each added item must be a different animal and have a different adjective. There is no need to stick too closely to nature in your descriptions, but it is sometimes as well to ban colours from the descriptions, as a child can go on for ever with these.

Prepositions
These are the words that describe where something is. Some are more difficult than others for a child to learn, and he usually begins with 'in,' 'on' and 'under'. Here are some ways of introducing them.

Treasure hunt
This game will take a little while to organise, so it is as well to set it up the evening before you want to play it with your child. Decide on about half a dozen hiding places around the house, or even in one room, and draw pictures as clues leading from one hiding place to another. For example, the first clue could show a picture of a chair with a big 'X' underneath the chair. The next clue would then be hidden under a chair, preferably stuck on with sticky tape so that it does not get lost. This clue could be a picture of a bookshelf with the 'X' on the shelf. Continue making up the clues in this way, using the simpler

'Treasure hunt': use clear illustrations for the clues

prepositions the first time you play, and perhaps introducing 'between', 'beside' or 'in front of' on later occasions. Put a small sweet, or some other 'treasure' in the final hiding place.

When you play the game, give the first clue to your child, and make him describe where he is going to look before he rushes

'Climbing': under the table

off. You can include as many children as you like in the game, but make sure there are enough prizes to go around. A 'treasure chest' full of chocolate buttons makes an appropriate multiple prize.

Climbing
Use a chair, or a small and very sturdy table for this game. Children enjoy playing it with a table, because this adds an element of 'naughtiness' but it is a good idea to establish at the outset that climbing on a table is only allowed during this game. Give your child instructions which include a preposition. At first, keep these simple, such as, 'Sit on the table,' or 'Sit under the table,' but after a while you can make it more complicated, including different actions as well as places. You might say, 'Stand behind the table on one leg,' or 'Lie down next to the table and sing a nursery rhyme.' Be brave and let your child give you some instructions as well.

Parking the car
Gather together a collection of toy cars, choosing ones which have marked differences from each other. They can be of different colours, sizes and makes. You may find you need to take your child's advice over the makes of the cars, as he is likely to know more about them than you do. Line the cars up and begin to give your child instructions as to where to park them – for example, 'Park the red one inside the garage.' Increase the complexity of the instructions as the game continues, so that you might say, 'Park the green one in front of the lorry, and the red one behind it.' If your child becomes enthusiastic about this game you can introduce all sorts of elements such as parking tickets and car smashes. Use a toy garage if you have one, or make one out of a cardboard box. Bear in mind that the main object of the game is to practise prepositions, so keep these well to the fore in your instructions.

Concept development
These games will help to widen and enrich your child's language by encouraging 'concept development'. There are many commercial games available which have the same purpose but the games described here deal with the ways you can link things

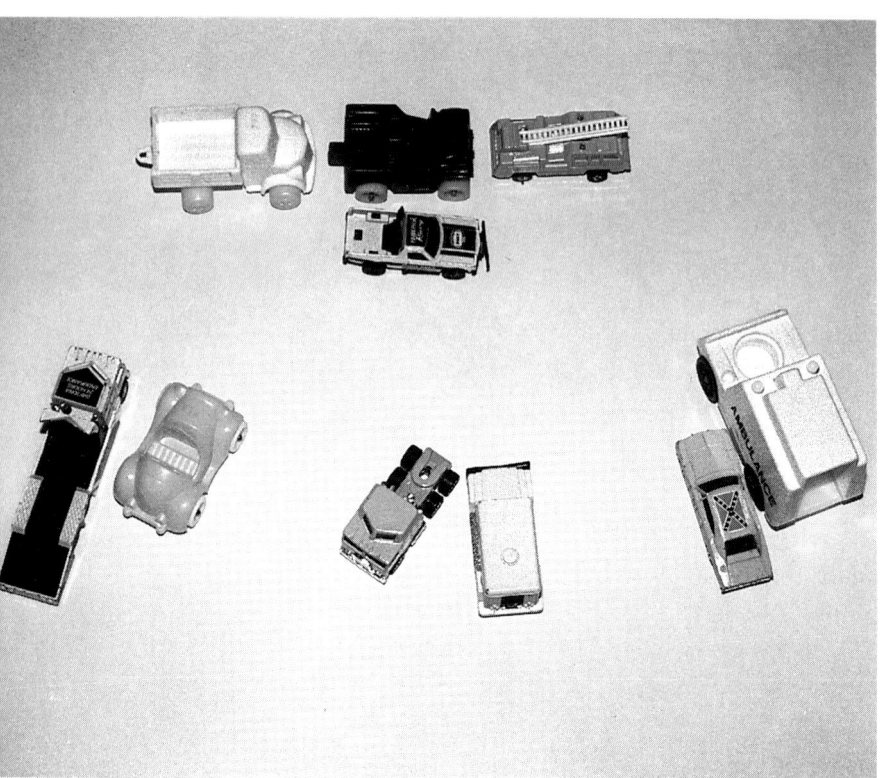

'Parking the car'

together and put them in categories, whilst at the same time noticing the differences between them.

Furniture
Use as large a sheet of paper or card as you can find, and draw lines to divide it into rooms. It is probably easiest to have just a kitchen, sitting room, dining room, bedroom and bathroom, but you can add any others that you like. Now get out your magazines and go through them with your child, hunting for pictures of furniture that you can cut out and stick on the

82

picture. You will find yourself needing to discuss things with your child, for example, which curtains or carpets to use, as you will find many pictures to choose from in the magazines. These discussions help him to use language effectively, and will introduce him to many new words. Treat him as an equal partner in these discussions.

Town planning
This is a large undertaking, and will take several days to complete. You will need as many boxes of varying sizes as you can find, as well as lolly sticks, cotton wool, plasticine, coloured pencils and tinfoil. In fact, throw nothing away for about a week before you intend to start this. You will also need a large board, or a table that you can manage without for a few days.

You and your child are going to make a model of a town, using the boxes for buildings. Help him to think of all the things that are needed in a town, including such things as houses, shops, parks, gardens and trees. You will have to use a good deal of ingenuity to make the models, but you will find your child has many ideas of his own for making them. The whole exercise not only introduces many different concepts and ideas, it also helps him to think in an ordered way and to carry through his own ideas. It is a really worthwhile project, but you will have to be prepared for a great deal of mess while it is going on.

Nature trail
Go for a walk in a park with your child, and let him collect anything interesting he can find. When you arrive home, help him to sort it all out into categories, so that each item goes with at least one other. You will find there are dozens of ways that you can group things, from putting all the leaves together, or all the yellow things, to matching a leaf with a piece of paper because you can tear them both, or a stone with a piece of wood because they are both hard. Let your child use his imagination.

'Nature trail': Choosing things to take home

Group the objects together in original ways

old

new

soft

short

hard

smooth

spiky

long

dull

shiny

SOUND GAMES

Before you begin to play games from this section with your child, you should have read the chapter entitled 'Speech sounds'. This explains something about how we make different sounds and the ways in which many of them are similar to each other. It also explains something of the order in which you might expect sounds to develop in your child's speech. The games in this section are intended to help your child to improve his ability to distinguish between different sounds and to improve the mobility of his articulators. This will make it easier for him to learn to make the sounds himself, but you should beware of trying to make him practise individual sounds, particularly in words, as a child can very quickly become upset and even unwilling to talk if he feels he is getting sounds wrong.

In order to make the best use of these games, it is helpful if you are aware of which sounds, or groups of sounds your child is using. Parents are often surprised to find that their child, who they thought was not using a [k] because he said 'tat' instead of 'cat', or 'tea' instead of 'key', is in fact using the [k] sound in many words, but in different positions. It is quite common for a [k] to appear first at the end of words such as 'book'. As a general rule of thumb, if your child is using a sound anywhere, in any word, he should eventually put it in the correct places.

So, before you begin the sound games, listen carefully to what your child says. Choose a group of sounds, such as those made with the lips, and listen to (and watch) him talking for a while to see if he is using any of those sounds. Make a note as to whether he seems to use them all easily, or uses none of them, or manages perhaps one but none of the others. Then move on to another group of sounds. Do not try to go through all the sounds at one session, and do not worry if you find it difficult to tell whether he is using sounds or not. None of the games will do him harm, so it is not essential, just helpful, that you know just what sounds he is making. You will find it easiest to listen properly to your child's speech if someone else is talking to him, or showing him pictures, so that you do not have to do too many things at once and can concentrate on listening. Do not ask him to repeat words if you are not sure whether or not he said them correctly. He should be blissfully unaware that you are listening to his speech. It can be very helpful if you tape record what he is saying. He will love listening to himself, and you will be able to listen to the tape again to check on which groups of sounds he is using. You will, however, probably be surprised to find how difficult it is to distinguish each sound when you hear the tape again. This shows how much you are lip-reading, and also how much more efficient the human ear is than a tape recorder!

If, having listened to your child's speech, you feel really concerned that he has very few sounds, or that he is using the wrong sounds in the wrong places, you should get in touch with your speech therapist to check on whether he needs more specific exercises than you can provide for him. If, however, you feel that his sounds are coming along reasonably happily, but that you would like to help him to improve more quickly, then play some games with him. The listening games from the section on language games will be useful to begin with, as they will encourage your child to listen carefully to sounds. When he can play some of them well, introduce some of the following games which deal with speech sounds.

Sound cards

The purpose of making these cards is to let you and your child play with the sounds we use in speech, without making him think too much about his speech and causing anxiety. You will want to use these cards many times, so make them carefully.

You will need plenty of cardboard, cut into large squares with sides of about six inches. Draw large, simple pictures (practise first on pieces of paper), paint or colour them, and cover them with transparent plastic. They will then be almost indestructible.

'Sound cards': think of the sound associated with the object, not its name

For each sound, choose a picture that represents the sound itself. Do not think about the spelling, but the sounds associated with the pictures. Here are a few examples.

[p]   a fish, gulping

[t]   a tap, dripping

[d]   a drum

[k]   a gun

[f]   a rabbit with protruding teeth

[s]   a snake, hissing

[ʃ]   a finger on some lips

[tʃ]   a train

These are just a few examples. The list of consonants in the Speech Sounds chapter shows the sounds that you will find most useful when playing sound games and you will be able to think up illustrations to go with them. It does not matter if the picture used is rather far-fetched, so long as you and your child agree that it stands for the sound.

Teach your child which card illustrates which sound by showing a card and saying the sound. Do not ask your child to say the sound, but if he does attempt it do not criticise the attempt. Begin with the sounds that children find the easiest, such as [p], [b], [t], [d]. When your child knows the cards for three or four sounds, you can begin to play some of the ear-training games.

Sound discrimination

The purpose of this game is to help your child distinguish between two or three different sounds. If you feel there is a particular group of sounds that your child is not using, it would be helpful to include one sound from this group in the game. Choose two other sounds, preferably ones that he is already using himself. Remember that he will be listening to the sounds, not saying them.

Put the three cards that illustrate the sounds you have chosen on the table in front of him, and give him a handful of counters. You say one of the sounds, ensuring that you say the sound, not the name of the sound. For example, [s] should be pronounced as a hiss, not as 'ess'. Let him put a counter on the sound card which corresponds to this sound. If he has no difficulty with this, tell him that you are going to 'hide' the sound inside a word, and say a word for him that contains one of the sounds. At first, use a word that features the sound at the beginning, but as he becomes more skilful, you can use words with the sound at the end, or in the middle. See figure 4 for examples of how a sound can appear in different positions in a word.

This sound discrimination game is the basis for much of the

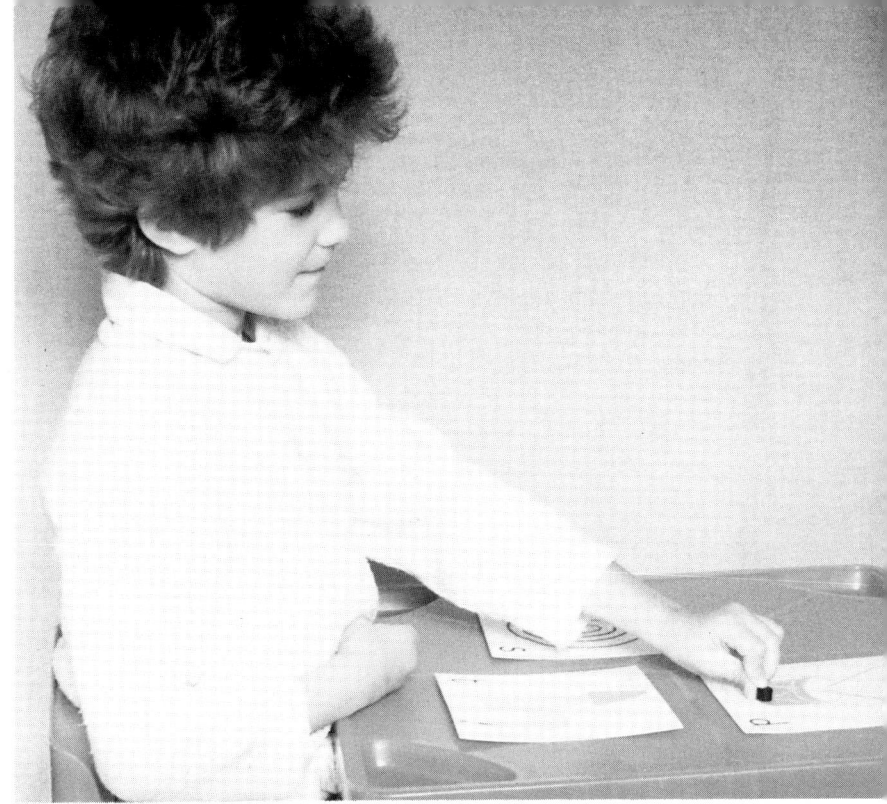

'Sound discrimination': careful listening to speech sounds helps your child learn to say them correctly

help you can give your child, as it encourages him to be aware of sounds and the differences between them, but it does not require him to make the sound himself. Vary the basic game with others so that your child always finds it enjoyable.

Sound posting box

Make up two or three posting boxes out of shoe boxes by painting them brightly and cutting slits in the lid. Then make some small picture cards, drawing pictures of things which begin with the sounds you have been using. For example, for the sound [p] you could use pictures of a pig, purse, pen, pin, penny, and post. For [t] you could use tea, toy, television, and teddy. As always, choose the words according to the sounds in them, not according to spelling. 'Thumb' for example, does not

89

begin with the sound [t] but with [θ]. Keep these cards separate from the large sound cards.

Find the appropriate large sound cards, make sure your child is familiar with them and lay them on the table. Stand a post box next to each of them. Then hand your child one of the small picture cards and say the word clearly, with a little emphasis on the relevant sound in the word. All your child has to do is to put the card through the correct posting box. He may want to make the sound or even say the word as he is posting the card. If he does, you should not correct his speech. Keep the emphasis of the game on listening.

Figure 4
A sound can appear in various places in a word

Sound	In initial position	In final position	In medial position
[p]	pig pie pan	hop up lip	open apple ripple
[s]	swing snake sand	house bus horse	poster aspirin master
[m]	man milk mountain	hum lamb comb	camera airman summer

Nonsense words
Put the whole pile of sound cards face down in front of your child. Say that you are going to make up some funny words beginning with, for example, 'ee'. You need to supply a vowel sound here. Say the vowel you have chosen, then let your child turn over the first card for you, so that you can join that sound on. This means that, if you have chosen 'ee', and the first card he turns over is the rabbit, for [f], you end up with the nonsense word, 'eef'.

If he is enthusiastic about the game and wants to have a go himself, then let him, but be uncritical about the result if he cannot make the sound correctly. Just repeat the nonsense word yourself, and go on to the next one. You may well find that your child can use sounds in this game that he is not yet using in his speech, because he is not thinking of the whole word but of individual sounds. So do not be surprised or disappointed if he does not at once transfer the sound into his speech. This will come in time.

I spy

Play the game of 'I Spy', but with the essential difference that you talk about sounds, not letters. Thus, you can say, 'I spy with my little eye, something beginning with [t].' Make sure that you say [t] and not 'tee'.

Right and wrong

Use a blackboard and some chalks for this game. Divide the board into two columns by drawing a chalk line down the centre, then draw one of the pictures from a sound card at the top left-hand column. Then draw the same picture at the top of the other column, and put a large cross through it. Give the chalk to your child and tell him to put a tick in the left-hand column when you say the sound correctly, and a cross in the right-hand column when you get it wrong.

Play this a few times, making the sound correctly sometimes and incorrectly at other times. When you are making it incorrectly, you can be as wildly wrong as you like. Try to make him laugh. Then rub out the pictures at the top of the columns, and replace them with pictures of a word which uses the sound at the beginning. Repeat the game, saying the whole word right or wrong. Go on to other sounds whenever you like. You will find your child will enjoy 'catching you out' as you say the sound incorrectly.

Naming the furniture

Put all the sound cards upside down in a pile on the table, then take the top one, show it to your child, say the sound and tell

91

him to put the card on top of something beginning with that sound. He could, for example, put the [t] card on top of a table, or the [s] card on top of a sock. You may find that he tries out the sound or the word as he does this. As usual, you should not criticise his attempt, just ensure that he hears you saying it correctly.

Sound blending
It is important that your child learns not only to make sounds correctly on their own, but also to string them together into words. You can help him to hear how to do this by playing the sound blending game. Draw pictures of two objects whose names sound almost the same. You could, for example, use 'cat' and 'cap', or any of the pairs from figure 3 (page 57). You then say one of the words, splitting it up into its component sounds. In this case you would say [k] – [a] – [t], leaving a tiny pause between each sound. Get your child to hold up the correct picture and say the word. He does not need to say each sound correctly, just say the whole word as best he can.

Once you have both got used to the game, you can stop using picture cards and just sound out the names of things around you, and see if he can guess the word. You will need to put in a little practice yourself so that you can split the word into its sounds easily. Remember to think about the sounds, and not the spelling of the word, as this can be very misleading. The word 'sugar' for example, begins with the sound [ʃ] or 'sh', rather than [s].

Tongue and lip exercises
When we talk, we are using the same organs that we use for feeding. This is why the development of a child's sucking and chewing skills are important to his eventual speech development. The chapter on Speech Sounds explains this relationship in more detail. It often happens that a child who was a 'messy feeder', or who dribbled a great deal in the first year or two of

life can continue to have slightly less control over his articulators than other children. This may lead to some lack of clarity in his speech as it develops.

In order to speak well, a child has to have a very exact control over what his tongue, lips and soft palate are doing. It is hard to duplicate the precise movements used in speech, except when saying words, but exercises can help a child to be more aware of what his articulators are doing, and can help him to achieve at least a minimum level of skill with sounds. This, combined with ear-training and some practice of sounds in isolation, will go some way towards better speech.

Lip exercises

To make many of the sounds of English, your child must be able to close his lips to prevent air escaping, so that the air can build up, to be released later with a small explosion. This happens with [p] and [b]. For [m] the lips must close so that air escapes only through the nose.

This closure takes place during eating, to prevent food from falling out of the mouth. Does your child sometimes dribble food when he is eating? If so, try these exercises.

Sit in front of a mirror with your child. Show him how to puff out his cheeks, then push the air out by banging his cheeks with his hands.

Stick a small piece of sticky tape on one of his lips, and tell him to get it off using his lips, not his hands or tongue.

Look in the mirror together, and see if he can make his lips disappear by pressing them together tightly.

Get out his toy cars and practise making 'Brrm brrm' noises.

Show your child how to make fish faces, by pushing his lips

forward, then opening and closing them without moving his cheeks.

Tongue exercises
In speech, the tongue is required to produce many tiny movements. Your child needs to be able to move the tongue tip up to the alveolar ridge, just behind the teeth, to move the back of the tongue up to the soft palate (for [k] and [g]), and to push the sides of the tongue up to the back teeth, leaving a channel in the middle for [s] and [ʃ], and let the sides of the tongue drop for [l]. It is impossible to duplicate all of these exactly in exercises, but the following ideas should produce some improvement.

Ask your child to count his teeth by touching each one with his tongue, beginning at the back of his top teeth and working his way around his mouth.

When he cleans his teeth, get him to feel around each of his

Puffing out their cheeks teaches children to close their lips tightly

teeth with his tongue afterwards to check that it is clean. If he has missed a bit his tooth will feel slightly rough.

Use a bottle of the kind of sauce sold for putting on top of ice-cream. Put a dab of it just above the centre of his top lip and let him lick it off with his tongue. Then put dabs of sauce in different places around his mouth so that his tongue is moving in all directions. Remember to make him clean his teeth as soon as he has tried this one.

Look in the mirror together, and try to put out your tongues without them touching your lips. You will probably find this as difficult as he does to begin with. Once you can achieve this feat, try to point the tips of your tongues and wobble them up and down as neatly as possible, again without touching your lips.

Soft palate exercises
The soft palate is the back of the roof of your mouth. It moves up and down during speech to allow air to escape either through the mouth, as in most sounds, or through the nose as in the nasal sounds [m], [n], and [ŋ]. If the palate is not moving effectively, there will be nasal escape of air during much of a child's speech, and the plosive sounds, such as [p], [b], [t], [k] etc. will sound muffled.

Get your child to blow hard through a trumpet, a party blower or a whistle. Ask him to blow his cheeks out as he does when exercising his lips. If air escapes down his nose it is likely that his palate is not sealing off the nasal passages sufficiently.

Give your child a straw and let him blow small pieces of paper off a table. Make sure that he doesn't cheat by not using the straw.

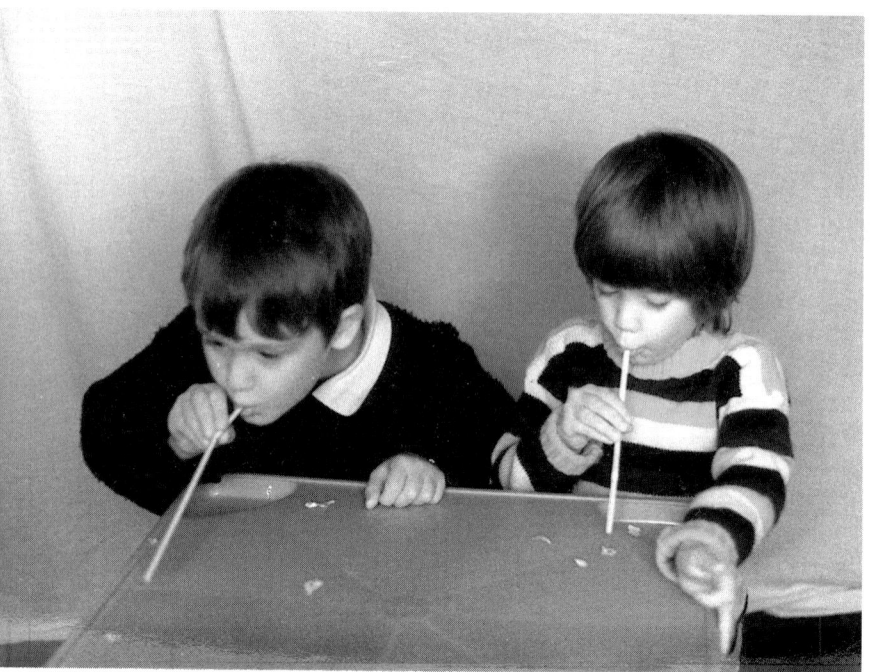

Blowing through a straw uses lip, cheek and soft palate muscles

Make bubble pictures with him. Put some water colour paint in a paper cup with plenty of water and a few drops of washing-up liquid. Put a straw in the cup and let him blow until there are plenty of bubbles on the surface of the water. Then put a sheet of paper on top of the bubbles. Lift it off and you should have a pattern of coloured circles on the paper. Make sure that your child is blowing and not sucking, or he will end up with a mouthful of paint!

Put large blobs of paint on a piece of paper, give your child a straw and let him blow on the blobs, which will spread over the paper. An attractive design can be produced by repeating the process with different colours.

VOICE GAMES

There are several simple ways in which your child can improve his control over his voice mechanisms. These will help to lay down good patterns which will stand him in good stead in later life.

Your child needs to use his full lung power often, so that he exercises the muscles and is less likely to fall into the bad habit of using only the top of his lungs. Posture is an important element here, as poor posture gives little room for the chest to expand, so that the lungs are not fully inflated. Children, however, do not respond favourably to being told to 'sit up straight'. You need a more subtle approach! Try to ensure that your child's chair is the right height for him when he is sitting at the table so that he does not have to stoop down to eat or to do his drawings. Give him a good model by remembering to sit and stand straight yourself. Point out and praise him for the times when you see him sitting or standing well.

Blow football

For this game, use straws and some paper which has been rolled up into a ball. Make sure before you begin that the paper ball is not too big and heavy to be moved by blowing through the straw.

Tell your child to kneel on the floor in front of a table. This table should be tall enough for your child's chin to be on the same level. This will keep his posture correct during the game. You go to the other side of the table, decide where the goal posts are to be, then compete with your child as to who can score the most goals by blowing the ball with a straw. Point out to him that a long, steady breath will be more effective than lots of short ones.

Balloons

Give him a balloon and tell him to see how long he can keep it up in the air by blowing, without using his hands. If there is another child there, you can make a race out of it. Stand each child behind a starting line, with a balloon, tell them where the finish is and let them race there. If a balloon touches the floor that child has to go back to the beginning again.

Singing competition

Have a competition with your child to see who can keep a note going longest. You can use just one sound, such as 'oo', or a word. Sing the notes loudly, as this will encourage him to keep a steady stream of breath going. You could organise the competition amongst several children, but be prepared for a great deal of noise.

Humming

Hum the tune of a nursery rhyme, and see if your child can guess which it is. Then let him have a turn. This encourages him to keep a good breath flow, and also to 'place' his voice correctly so that he makes full use of his resonators.

Kazoo

A kazoo is a kind of musical instrument which works on the 'comb and paper' principle. Whoever is playing it needs to produce a good voice before it will work, so it is useful voice practice for your child. Most toy shops sell kazoos very cheaply.

Whistles

A whistle is blown using the breath alone, without voice. If you can bear it, give your a child a whistle, have one yourself and see who can blow the longest note. Then see who can blow the quietest note, as this requires more breath control.

Singing

If you and your child enjoy singing, it is a very useful way to exercise his voice. Make sure he is standing or sitting well when

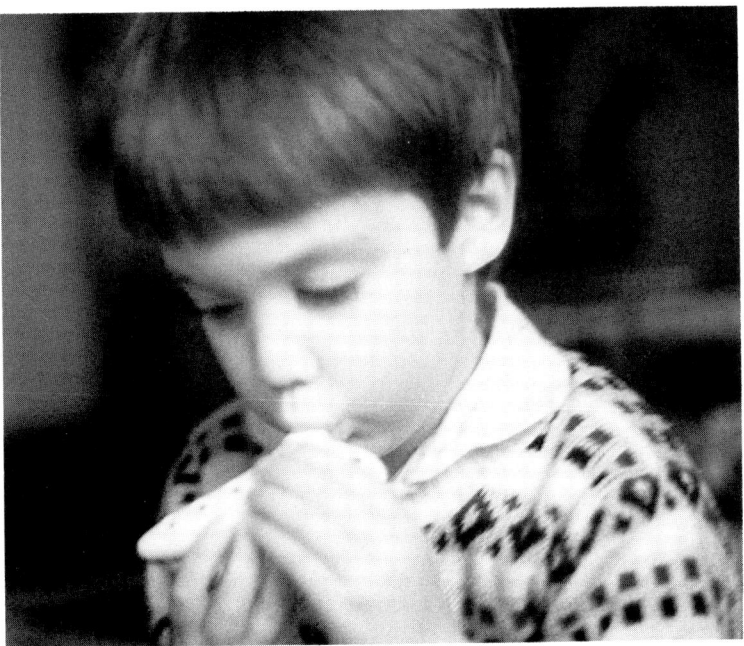

Long notes blown on a whistle improve breath control

you sing together, but do not let him become self-conscious. Sing a familiar song with him, and see how much of the song he can manage without taking more than one breath. Sing it in a high voice, then sing it again in a low voice, to encourage pitch changes. If he learns to carry over some of the features of singing, such as the variations in pitch, to his speech, his voice will become far more interesting and pleasant for the listener.

Further help

Parents who, having read this book, feel they would like to know more about language development in children would do well to read *Listen to Your Child: A Parent's Guide to Children's Language* by David Crystal (Penguin Books Ltd, 1986). This explains the process of language acquisition in more detail than has been possible here.

If a child has enjoyed the games in this book, and is talking well, he may also enjoy some of the pre-reading and reading games to be found in *Reading Through Play: The Easy Way to Teach Your Child* by Carol Baker (Macdonald & Co 1980).

Information on any aspect of speech therapy can be obtained from:

The College of Speech Therapists,
Harold Poster House,
6 Lechmere Road,
London NW2 5BU

The Association for All Speech Impaired Children (AFASIC) will give support, advice and help to parents. They can be contacted at:

AFASIC,
347 Central Markets,
Smithfield,
London EC1A 9NH

Other associations that exist for the benefit of the speech handicapped include:

Invalid Children's Aid Nationwide (ICAN),
198 City Road,
London EC1V 2PH

(This organisation produces a newsletter called 'Speech and Language Disorders News'.)

VOCAL,
South Western Hospital,
St Peter's Office,
Landor Road,
London SW9

AFS (Association For Stammerers),
c/o Finsbury Centre,
Pine Street,
London EC1R 0JH

INDEX

References to illustrations are printed in **bold-face** type.